Historic Cumnock

the archaeological implications of development

E P Dennison **Torrie**

Russel **Coleman**

the Scottish burgh survey

HISTORIC SCOTLAND

in association with

SCOTTISH CULTURAL PRESS

CENTRE FOR SCOTTISH URBAN HISTORY
Department of Scottish History
University of Edinburgh

Strathclyde

CUMNOCK AND DOON VALLEY
DISTRICT COUNCIL

publication	Historic Scotland *in association with* Scottish Cultural Press First published 1995
copyright	© Historic Scotland 1995 *The moral right of the authors has been asserted.*
editorial	Olwyn Owen
design	Christina Unwin
printing . binding	British Printing Company, Aberdeen
ISSN	1358 0272
Scottish Cultural Press ISBN	1 898218 40 4
all distribution and sales enquiries	Scottish Cultural Press PO Box 106 Aberdeen AB9 8ZE telephone *01224* 583777 . facsimile *01224* 575337
all other enquiries	■ Scottish burgh surveys Centre for Scottish Urban History Department of Scottish History University of Edinburgh EH8 9LN telephone *0131* 650 4032 . facsimile *0131* 650 4032 ■ Historic Scotland Longmore House Salisbury Place Edinburgh EH9 1SH telephone *0131* 668 8600 . facsimile *0131* 668 8699
British Library cataloguing in publication data	A catalogue record for this book is available from the British Library

contents

This account of the history and archaeology of Cumnock is one of a series of reports on the historic burghs of Scotland—known collectively as the *Scottish Burgh Survey*—all of which have been commissioned by **Historic Scotland** and its predecessors. Some 56 burghs have been surveyed during previous campaigns of the Scottish Burgh Survey (1978–90). *Historic Cumnock* is only the third survey to have been formally published (the first two were *Historic Kirkcaldy* and *Historic Stranraer*).

Since it was created a burgh of barony by James IV in 1509, with its strategic position at the meeting-point of important routes, Cumnock has played host to many over the years—hence the large number of historic inns and hotels it boasts. Cumnock was founded initially to provide one of the king's favoured local subjects, James Dunbar, with a market. The original site of the market cross (and market place) has been a matter of some debate—and is one of the mysteries this survey may have solved. Cumnock's later history is dominated by the Covenanters, the Cumnock pottery and Keir Hardie, among other things. The architectural importance of Cumnock's historic core has previously been recognised in the designation of the Square as a Conservation Area. Now this survey highlights the potential survival of archaeological evidence for Cumnock's historic past.

The main aim of *Historic Cumnock* is to identify those areas in the historic burgh which are of archaeological interest and therefore require sensitive treatment in the event of any proposed development or other ground disturbance. It is designed primarily as a working manual for the use of local authorities and archaeological curators. However, as an essential prerequisite to this assessment of the archaeological implications of development, it also describes and illustrates the geography and geology of the town, its known archaeology and history, its historic standing buildings and the origins of its street names—all of which will be of interest to the wider public, be they inhabitant, visitor or student.

Publication of the Scottish Burgh Survey is part of an initiative to analyse and make widely available all the known archaeological and historical information about Scotland's historic burghs, at a time when many of them are continuing to experience development and other pressures. As the relevant local bodies work to ensure the continuing viability of historic town centres whilst also safeguarding their heritage through sensitive conservation policies, individual burgh surveys are intended to contribute to their work in a practical way. They also remind a wider audience of the importance and vulnerability of historic town centres. The delicate balance between sustainable development and heritage conservation is not a new dilemma in historic towns; residents and local authorities have been grappling with similar issues on and off over the centuries—the levelling of the graveyard in the Square in Cumnock in the mid eighteenth century to provide access for wheeled traffic, is a case in point.

Historic Cumnock was prepared for Historic Scotland within the **Centre for Scottish Urban History**, which is part of the Department of Scottish History, University of Edinburgh. Dr E P Dennison Torrie, Director of the Centre for Scottish Urban History, and Russel Coleman, of the **Scottish Urban Archaeological Trust**, are co-authors of the report. Kevin Hicks, of the **Centre for Field Archaeology**, University of Edinburgh, is cartographer and illustrator, and Alan MacDonald of the Department of Scottish History acted as research assistant. The project is supervised by the Head of the Department, Professor Michael Lynch, and managed for Historic Scotland by Olwyn Owen, Inspector of Ancient Monuments.

The survey of historic Cumnock was entirely funded by Historic Scotland. This report has been published with financial assistance from **Cumnock and Doon Valley District Council**, **Strathclyde Regional Council** and Historic Scotland. Further copies may be obtained from **Scottish Cultural Press**, PO Box 106, Aberdeen AB9 8ZE.

cover notes

Extract from Roy's military survey, 1747–55 (by permission of The British Library). At the age of 20, William Roy (1726–1790) was appointed assistant to Lieutenant-Colonel David

Watson, who was under the immediate orders of the Duke of Cumberland to extend Marshal Wade's plan for the subjection of the clans by opening up communication through the Scottish highlands. In 1747, when Roy was superintending road-building by the troops, he helped Watson to prepare the map known as the Duke of Cumberland's map of mainland Scotland, but it would be more accurately described as a magnificent military sketch. At a later date the map was reduced by Watson and Roy, engraved in a single sheet and published as the king's map. Roy's love of archaeology, which was to endure throughout his life, showed itself in the insertion of Roman names and camps. This extract clearly shows the Square of mid eighteenth-century old Cumnock.

vi   acknowledgements

Thanks go to the staff of the **District History Centre and Baird Institute Museum, Cumnock**. Mr John Laurenson, Local History Librarian, and Mr Charlie Woodward, Community Museums' Development Officer were particularly helpful. The assistance of **Cumnock and Doon Valley District Council Department of Planning** was also gratefully received.

Staff of the **Scottish Urban Archaeological Trust** have been supportive, and colleagues at the **University of Edinburgh** have given valuable support and advice. In particular, we would like to mention the **Centre for Field Archaeology**.

The assistance given by the **Royal Commission on the Ancient and Historical Monuments of Scotland** has been particularly useful, especially that of Dr Iain Fraser. We are indebted to Mrs Lily Linge and Ms Deirdre Cameron of **Historic Scotland**. We would like also to acknowledge the assistance of Dr Carol Swanson and Mr Hugh McBrien of **Strathclyde Region Archaeological Service**.

The staff of the **Scottish Record Office** and of the **National Library of Scotland**, at both George IV Bridge and the Map Library at Causewayside, have been extremely helpful.

To all of these we extend our thanks.

figure 2 is reproduced by kind permission of the **Ministry of Defence**. © *Crown Copyright*: MOD.

figures 3 & **8** are reproduced by kind permission of the **Trustees of the National Library of Scotland**.

figures 4–7, 10–12 & **16–21** are reproduced by kind permission of **the District History Centre, Baird Institute, Cumnock and Doon Valley District Council**.

figure 9 is reproduced by kind permission of **The British Library**.

figures 1 & **13–16** are based upon the 1986–88 Ordnance Survey 1:10,000 scale and the Ordnance Survey 1:2,500 map series, with permission of **The Controller of Her Majesty's Stationery Office**. © *Crown Copyright*.

abbreviations		
APS	*The Acts of The Parliaments of Scotland*, 12 vols, edd T Thomson & C Innes (Edinburgh, 1814–75).	
CDS	*Calendar of Documents Relating to Scotland*, 5 vols, ed J Bain *et al* (Edinburgh, 1881–8, 1986).	
DES	*Discovery and Excavation in Scotland.*	
ER	*The Exchequer Rolls of Scotland*, 23 vols, edd J Stuart *et al* (Edinburgh, 1878–1908).	
Macfarlane, *Geog Colls*	Walter Macfarlane, *Geographical Collections Relating to Scotland*, ed A Mitchell, 3 vols (SHS, 1906–8).	
NLS	National Library of Scotland, Edinburgh.	
NSA	*The New Statistical Account of Scotland* (Edinburgh, 1845).	
OSA	*The Statistical Account of Scotland 1791–1799*, ed Sir John Sinclair, New edition, edd D.J Withrington & I R Grant (Wakefield, 1973).	
PPS	Proceedings of the Prehistoric Society.	
PSAS	Proceedings of the Society of Antiquaries of Scotland.	
RCRB	*The Records of the Convention of Royal Burghs of Scotland*, 7 vols, ed J D Marwick (Edinburgh, 1866–1918).	
RCAHMS	The Royal Commission on the Ancient and Historical Monuments of Scotland.	
RMS	*The Register of the Great Seal of Scotland (Registrum Magni Sigilli Regum Scotorum)*, 11 vols, edd J M Thomson *et al* (Edinburgh, 1882–1914).	
RPC	*The Register of the Privy Council of Scotland*, edd J H Burton *et al* (Edinburgh, 1877–).	
RRS	*Regesta Regum Scottorum*, 6 vols, edd G W S Barrow *et al* (Edinburgh, 1960–).	
SHS	Scottish History Society.	
SRO	Scottish Record Office, Edinburgh.	
TDGNHAS	*Transactions of the Dumfries and Galloway Natural History and Antiquarian Society.*	

1   Use the colour coded map on the foldout at the back of this book **figure 22** and/or the **general index** to locate a particular site (normally the site of a development proposal).

2   If the site is in a **blue area**, any development proposal is unlikely to affect significant archaeological remains. No action is needed.

3   **Green areas** are designated as potentially archaeologically sensitive. If the site is in a green area, it is possible that a proposal involving ground disturbance may encounter archaeological remains. Seek appropriate archaeological advice as early as possible.

4   **Red areas** are Scheduled Ancient Monuments or properties in the care of the Secretary of State for Scotland, and are protected by law. Consult Historic Scotland.

5   Use the map on p 26 **figure 13** to determine into which area of the burgh the site falls (Area 1 or 2), and turn to the relevant area in the **area by area assessment** for a fuller account (pp 27–37).

6   Use the **general index** and, if appropriate, the listing of **street names** (pp 53–4) for rapid access to information specific to a site, street or named feature of the town.

step 1

As a working manual, the first point of reference is the colour-coded map at the back of the book **figure 22**.

The **red areas** are **protected by law**. All applications for planning consent must be referred to Historic Scotland acting for the Secretary of State in terms of Section 15(j)(v) of the Town and Country Planning (General Development Procedure) (Scotland) Order 1992. All enquiries regarding prospective development proposals in red areas should be referred to Historic Scotland for advice at as early a stage as possible.

The **green areas** are **potentially archaeologically sensitive** and may retain significant sub-surface archaeological information. Consultation should take place with the local authority archaeologist, where any development proposal or enquiry involving ground disturbance is being considered, including car parks, road schemes, environmental improvements, landscaping and drainage schemes, as well as the usual range of development and re-development proposals in built-up areas. There is no necessity for a consultation where ground disturbance is not in prospect, such as applications for change of use of a building. If in doubt whether consultation is necessary, please refer to the local authority archaeologist. It is important to note that sub-surface disturbance within historic standing buildings may also affect archaeological remains, and that some standing buildings may retain archaeological features within their structures. Please seek advice as required.

The **blue areas** denote those parts of the historic burgh which **may be archaeologically sterile** and where archaeological consultation is probably not necessary. In practice, there is rarely a hard dividing line between the green and the blue areas. If in any doubt, check the account of the relevant area in the **area by area assessment** (*see* step 2), and seek archaeological advice as appropriate.

step 2

In this new series of burgh surveys, each survey has been organised locationally, in order to assist speedy consultation on any proposed development site. In the case of Cumnock, the

2

historic core of the town has been divided into two arbitrary areas, Areas 1 and 2, which are shown on the plan on p 26 **figure 13**. The second step for the user, then, is to consult this plan and to determine into which area a specific enquiry falls.

step 3

Both areas are assessed individually in the **area by area assessment** (pp 27–37). The commentary for each area is prefaced with a detailed plan of that area. Archaeological, historical, geographical and geological factors of particular relevance to the area are all discussed, and an assessment of the archaeological potential is made. For ease of reference, even if a dividing line between areas is shown as the middle of a street, discussion of the area includes any elements within the street up to the opposite frontage. The importance of an integrated approach to the historical and archaeological information is implicit in the design of this report: the history and archaeology are presented together on each page rather than consecutively.

This integrated, area-based approach has involved some repetition of information in the area by area assessment, in order that users are not required to cross-reference more than necessary when dealing with a specific enquiry. Although such repetition would not be normal in a work of interest to the general public, it was felt that it would be permissible here in order to facilitate the work of primary users: local authority planners and other curators of the archaeological resource.

historic standing buildings

historic buildings reinforces the above sections by providing basic historical and architectural information about the historic standing buildings of the town; where relevant, it also provides the area location and an assessment of the archaeological potential of specific buildings. *It should always be borne in mind that historic standing buildings may also contain archaeological remains, both beneath their floors and within their structures.*

objectives for future fieldwork and research

Any report of this nature cannot be definitive. During its preparation, a series of archaeological and historical objectives for future fieldwork and research have been identified; these are listed at pp 47–8. They will be of particular interest to urban historians and archaeologists, and to those responsible for management of the archaeological resource in historic Cumnock.

referencing

The report contains a comprehensive **general index** as well as a listing of **street names** giving basic historical information and, where relevant, area location. A **bibliography** and a **glossary** of technical terms have also been included, as well as a summary of chance finds from in and around the burgh.

The data accumulated during preparation of this survey and draft copies of the completed work, as well as any unpublished reports of any small-scale excavations and watching briefs, are housed in the **National Monuments Record**, John Sinclair House, 16 Bernard Terrace, Edinburgh EH8 9NX, telephone *0131* 662 1456, facsimile *0131* 662 1477/1499.

full reference to this report   Torrie, E P Dennison and Coleman, R 1995 *Historic Cumnock: the archaeological implications of development*, published by Historic Scotland in association with Scottish Cultural Press, Aberdeen. (Scottish Burgh Survey 1995).

the Scottish burgh survey

4

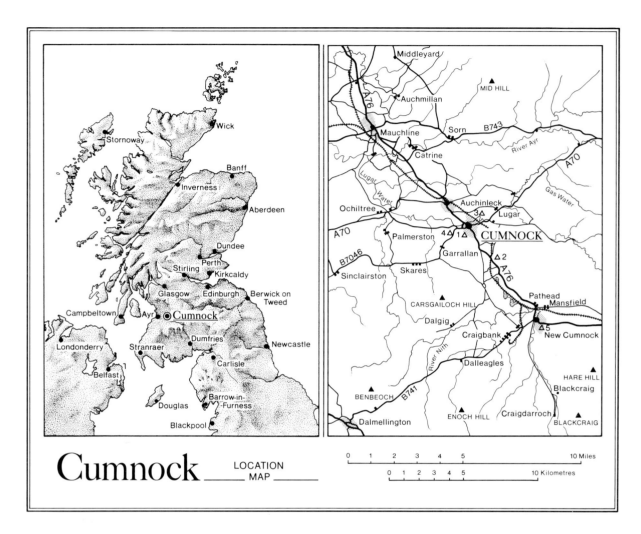

Cumnock

LOCATION MAP

figure 1

Location of Cumnock

**Cumnock:
its site
and setting**

Cumnock stands on a slight plateau, 125 m above sea-level, in a small valley formed by the Lugar and Glaisnock Waters. The Lugar, which starts at the confluence of the Glenmuir and Bella Waters some 3 km above the town, meets the Glaisnock (which flows from the Black Loch about 3 km distant to the south) within the old burgh boundary, and then flows west to join the River Ayr near Mauchline. The burgh also holds a strategic position at the meeting-point of important routes, east to west between Ayr and Edinburgh, and north to south between Glasgow and the Nithsdale/Borders region **figure 1**.

On the medieval map, Cumnock's nearest neighbour was Auchinleck, 2 km to the north-west. Others were Mauchline (10 km), Ayr (22 km), Douglas (28 km) and Sanquhar (23 km). The castle of Cumnock, of which only a portion of the moat survives, lies some 8 km to the south. A number of other castles such as Leifnoreis (fifteenth century), Borland Castle (fourteenth century), and Terringzean Castle (late fourteenth to early fifteenth century), all lie within a radius of 3 km of the town.

Today, the largest of the towns of Ayrshire are Ayr and Kilmarnock, both with populations of around 50,000. On or near the coast are a string of sizeable towns—Largs, West Kilbride, Ardrossan, Saltcoats, Stevenston, Kilwinning, Troon, Prestwick and Girvan. Apart from Kilmarnock, Cumnock is the biggest local centre inland, with a population of nearly 10,000.[1]

The rolling landscape of the area is punctuated by stretches of woodland against a backdrop of the moorlands beyond. The empty moors and hills which surround the county on its landward sides almost entirely segregate Ayrshire from the adjoining counties. This means that Ayrshire has retained much of its sense of identity despite the legislative changes of 1975, which incorporated the area into the massive Strathclyde Region.[2] From April 1996, Cumnock will come within the area of the new East Ayrshire Council.

geology

South-east Scotland, like the rest of northern Britain, has a long and complex geological history with a wide variety of rocks and physical features. Tectonic movements along two major dislocations of the earth's crust, the Southern Uplands Fault and the Highland Boundary Fault, have created three principal structural and physiographic divisions—the Highlands, the Midland Valley and the Southern Uplands.[3]

The Midland Valley of Scotland, within which Cumnock lies, is the name given to the relatively low-lying central part of Scotland—lying between the Grampian Highlands and the Southern Uplands. It is defined geologically to the north by the Highland Boundary Fault, which extends from Stonehaven in the north-east to the Firth of Clyde at Helensburgh. Its limit in the south is the Southern Uplands Fault, which lies parallel to the Highland Boundary Fault and extends from Dunbar through New Cumnock to Glen App.[4] Although referred to as the Midland Valley, the region is rather more diverse than the name suggests. Much of it consists of farmland lying below *c* 180 m, but there are many upland areas of rough pasture and moorland.[5]

In south Lanarkshire and eastern Ayrshire a large area of dissected high ground extends from around the hilltop at Tinto (707 m) south-west to New Cumnock and northwards to Strathaven.[6] Much of the rest of the Midland Valley consists of areas of undulating lowland underlain by strata of Devonian and Carboniferous age (300–400 million years ago). The two largest lowland areas are central Ayrshire from Ardrossan to Ayr and extending inland to Kilmarnock and Cumnock, and the central belt from the Glasgow area to the Firth of Forth and into Fife and East Lothian. This undulating lowland landscape is enhanced by conspicuous landmarks formed of intrusive sheets or plugs of igneous rock (such as North Berwick Law; Traprain Law near Haddington; the castle rocks of Stirling and Edinburgh; and Dumbarton Rock).[7] Nearer to home, the cores of three extinct volcanoes survive in Ayrshire as impressive monuments of the geological past—Loudon Hill near Darvel; the Heads of Ayr; and the island of Ailsa Craig off Girvan.[8]

The lower-lying land of central Ayrshire rests on Carboniferous strata, with extensive beds of coals and limestones, which dip down to sea level. The youngest rocks of all, the red Permian sandstones found around Mauchline, were once quarried for house-building locally and even for export across the Atlantic.[9]

soils

The soils around Cumnock are derived from Carboniferous sediments and basic igneous rocks. These ancient rocks were crushed during the Ice Age into boulder clay which, as the glaciers melted, were left behind as a soil covering. On the uplands this remains as a thin layer, but lower down there are thicker deposits and an irregular surface of ridges, hillocks and valleys, which give the landscape its distinctive character.[10] To the south of Cumnock the principal drift is a grey clayey till, but some very strong sandy loam water-worked materials are also present. To the north the drift is derived from Carboniferous sediments, shales and limestones. Finally, fluvioglacial sands are present to the east and west, visible in the landscape as a series of mounds and terraces.[11]

climate and land use

The climate in Ayrshire is fairly warm to cool and wet with average rainfall of 1250 to 1500 mm per annum.[12] The rain, which contributes to the greenery of the Ayrshire landscape, may be expected throughout the year. While the months from April to July can be drier, August is often wet. The prevailing wind is a warm south-westerly, and the sea, which keeps things cool in summer, has a similar modifying effect in providing Ayrshire with mild winters—so mild indeed that palm trees grow at sheltered spots along the coast.[13]

The land is capable of producing a narrow range of crops and is suitable for enterprises based primarily on grassland with short arable breaks (*eg* barley, oats, forage crops). Yields of arable crops are variable because of soil, wetness or climatic factors; yields of grass are often high but difficulties of production or utilisation may be encountered. Limitations, such as wetness, occasional flooding, and shallow or stony soils restrict the choice of crops and demand careful management.[14] On the lowlands, however, where there is less rain and a longer growing season, generations of liming and draining and hard work by farmers have made Ayrshire a noted agricultural region.[15]

Tree planting has been carried out in the hills and uplands of the western and central Midland Valley by Muirkirk, Cumnock and Darvel.[16] Coals, ironstones, limestones and oil-shales have been extensively worked; they formed the basis of the industrialisation of the Midland Valley during the nineteenth century and the first part of the twentieth century.[17]

topography and the physical setting of the burgh **figure 2**

The relationship between local topography and the morphology of the medieval burgh is important for this study. Firstly, it highlights the impact of the physical environment on first settlement, and the constraints it imposed on the subsequent development of the burgh. Secondly, it may help to pinpoint the original nucleus of settlement.

The burgh of Cumnock lies within the confluence of the Lugar and Glaisnock Waters **figure 2**. These two natural features provided physical boundaries to the extent of the early settlement and at the same time afforded a measure of defence and security. A third natural feature also figures heavily in the relationship between the natural topography and the development of the burgh. A steep hill (150 m OD) dominates the eastern end of the town (Hillside), which curves around the foot of the slope at between 110 m and 115 m OD. All three natural features must have defined the limits of the medieval burgh and restricted its expansion (*see* p 48).

figure 2
Cumnock from the air
1988
© *Crown Copyright:*
MOD

Modern-day Cumnock gives little impression of the character of the medieval townscape. Only a handful of burgage plots are preserved within the burgh and many of the streets have been widened. The cartographic sources indicate that the burgage plots that extended southwards from Townhead to the Glaisnock were long, and took advantage of the more gentle slope. On the opposite side, those that extended northwards up the hill were shorter, but perhaps wider. Whether plots extended all the way down to the Lugar or the Glaisnock is not clear—and any that did would have been in danger of flooding. Similarly, the slope to the north of Lugar Street may also have restricted the length of burgage plots. Terracing can be seen behind the Townhead Street and Lugar Street frontages.

Little is known of the layout of the burgh before the beginning of the eighteenth century. Today, it essentially comprises the Square and a number of converging routeways. The Square sits at the foot of the hill (Hillside), on a small plateau which falls away westwards down towards the Lugar Water, and southwards down to the Glaisnock Water. This is the focus of the town, and perhaps always has been. However, the Square originally consisted of the parish church surrounded by the graveyard, with a number of properties backing onto it. With the remodelling which took place throughout the eighteenth and nineteenth centuries, and the more recent pedestrianisation scheme, properties on all sides now face onto the Square (*see* p 17).

Many roads converge on the Square, or more accurately at Townhead (the western end of Townhead Street). This crossroads must always have been one of the busiest parts of the town, and therefore could have been the original site of the market cross (*see* **figure 15**).

notes

1   J Strawhorn and K Andrew *Discovering Ayrshire* (Edinburgh, 1994), 1.

2   *Ibid*, 5–6.

3   C J Brown & B M Shipley, *Soil Survey of Scotland: South-East Scotland*, 1:2500 000 Sheet 7. Soil and Land Capability for Agriculture (The Macaulay Institute for Soil Research, Aberdeen, 1982), 2. The three major land divisions (Highlands, Midland Valley and Southern Uplands) follow J B Sissons, *The Geomorphology of the British Isles: Scotland* (London, 1976).

4   I B Cameron & D Stephenson, *The Midland Valley of Scotland* (British Regional Geology, Natural Environment Research Council, 3rd edn, London, 1985), 1.

5   *Ibid*, 1.

6   *Ibid*, 2.

7   *Ibid*, 3.

8   J Strawhorn & K Andrew, *Discovering Ayrshire* (Edinburgh, 1994), 2.

9   *Ibid*, 1–2.

10 *Ibid*, 2.

11 Brown & Shipley, *Soil Survey of Scotland: South-East Scotland*.

12 *Ibid*.

13 Strawhorn & Andrew, *Discovering Ayrshire*, 4.

14 Brown & Shipley, *Soil Survey of Scotland: South-East Scotland*.

15 Strawhorn & Andrew, *Discovering Ayrshire*, 3.

16 F T Dry & J A Hipkin, *Land Capability for Forestry in South-East Scotland* (Macaulay Land Use Research Institute, Aberdeen, 1989), 8.

17 Cameron & Stephenson, *Midland Valley of Scotland*, 6.

archaeological and historical background

Relatively little archaeological work has been undertaken within the historic core of Cumnock, and few stray finds have been reported. However, a number of prehistoric, early historic, medieval and post-medieval finds have been recorded from a small area around the burgh. An introduction to the prehistory, Roman period and early historic history of the area has therefore been included, in order to place the finds in some sort of context and to provide a broader framework within which to study the origins of the medieval burgh. A summary of the conclusions from the area by area assessment of the burgh can be found on pp 33–9, and a gazetteer of all previous work and chance finds from within and around the burgh on pp 49–52.

prehistory

It was against a background of complex climatic fluctuations, such as rising and falling ocean levels, that the first settlement of Scotland took place, around 7,000 BC. At this time, during the Mesolithic period (literally, the Middle Stone Age), much of Scotland was covered in dense woodland, which supported a rich variety of game, particularly red deer.

Few settlements are known in Scotland from this period, but those that have been identified cluster along the coastline and river banks. These communities exploited marine resources, such as fish and shellfish, and followed the herds of woodland game through the seasons, while supplementing their diet with wild plants and berries. This semi-nomadic existence has left little trace in the archaeological landscape in the form of structural evidence, but shell middens and flints are common finds.

Changes in the environment, including an improvement in soil conditions, together with ideas introduced from continental Europe around 3,500 BC, allowed the transition from a hunter-gatherer society to a more settled existence based on farming. Large areas of woodland were cleared, partly by burning but also by cutting down trees with stone axes; livestock was kept and the land was farmed for crops. Again, relatively few traces of these Neolithic (New Stone Age) settlements survive, but the landscape still bears testament to their presence in the form of ritual enclosures or henges, and burial mounds.

Nowhere is ritual more strongly evident in the lives of these early farming groups than in their treatment of the dead and the arrangements made for burial. Amongst the earliest evidence for burial rites are small monumental tombs, or chambered cairns, often stone-built in western parts of Britain, but elsewhere constructed of wood and turf. Few have been identified in Ayrshire but a good example of a chambered tomb can be seen at Balmalloch, south-east of Girvan (NX 264 845).[1] There is considerable regional variation in the types and styles of these monuments, no doubt reflecting regional traditions and, perhaps, the origins of the peoples who built and used them.[2] These tombs may also have become a focus for ritual, perhaps with elaborate ceremonies being performed there to commemorate the ancestors.

By about 2,500 BC, changes in society were gradually taking place. The tradition of monumental tombs and the cult of the ancestors declined and, in its stead, came more community-oriented monuments, most of them no less enigmatic, such as the stone circles and standing stones of the late Neolithic and Bronze Age periods. These have excited a range of mathematical and astronomical interpretations and clearly incorporated in their design an awareness of the rising and setting of the sun and moon.[3]

In marked contrast to the earlier monumental tombs, which could contain large numbers of burials, a new trend was emerging of single grave burials. These often contained objects or grave goods. These were placed in the grave, perhaps for the afterlife, by relatives or those taking part in the funeral ceremony. They have also been interpreted as reflecting the position of the individual within the overall social hierarchy. A number of Bronze-Age burials, all in cinerary urns, have been found in and around Cumnock. In this particular tradition, the body was cremated, and the ashes contained in an urn. The urn may then have been placed within a small stone-lined cist set beneath a stone cairn, or in a pit. Very often the cairn has been removed, leaving only the cist. Some of these were single, isolated burials, but others, such as those at Borland Mill (NS 5855 1738), were part of a larger cemetery. Muirkirk, some 10 km north-east of Cumnock, is particularly rich in Bronze-Age burials, and a number of cemeteries, representing different traditions, have been found.[4]

During this period the manufacture of bronze weapons and artefacts became more skilled, with increasingly elaborate designs appearing and overall production increasing. The craftsmen themselves, perhaps travelling from place to place, must have held a high position within society. The individuals who commissioned them began to use the objects themselves as confirmation of their own authority, in what has been termed a 'prestige goods economy'. However, increasing numbers of valuable objects began to circulate, which devalued them, and their owners. To compensate, large quantities of metalwork were taken out of circulation, deposited either as offerings to the gods or spirits, or as grave goods. This had the dual effect of reducing the amount of valuable objects in circulation and reaffirming the position of the established hierarchy. The hoard of metalwork found at Sykeside Bridge (NS 5878 1913) may represent one of these offerings, although the exact details of this find are vague.

The end of the Bronze Age, around 600 BC, marks a period of considerable change, not only in the technological advances made, but also in the nature of society itself. Iron tools, and, increasingly, weapons, begin to appear in the archaeological record. Despite the abundance of evidence for large monuments and rich burials in the Neolithic and Bronze Age, knowledge of the subsistence base which supported these societies, and the settlements in which they lived, is rather poor.[5] However, by the late Bronze Age and early Iron Age, the position is reversed and domestic settlements begin to dominate the archaeological landscape. Numerous fortified settlements appear, ranging from large hillforts to enclosed villages and isolated single family dwellings. Although other, less defensive types of settlements also existed, the apparent preference for fortified settlements seems generally to reflect the emergence of a more competitive society—one which perhaps competed for natural resources as well as territory—and a movement away from the large monuments of the second and third millennia BC which served the community, to settlement types indicative of more tribal divisions.[6] A number of hillforts can be seen in Ayrshire, including Harpercroft (NS 360 325) and Wardlaw (NS 359 327), less than a quarter of a kilometre apart.[7]

the later prehistoric and Roman period

It was this fragmented society which the Romans encountered in the first century AD. They promptly established a network of fortifications and communications throughout southern Scotland which ensured their effective control of the native tribes. According to Ptolemy, the classical geographer writing in the second century AD, Ayrshire was then in the domain of the Dumnonii tribe.

Little is known about Roman activity in Ayrshire during this period, and few sites have been identified. The seemingly isolated fort at Loudon Hill (NS 60 37), approximately 20 km north of Cumnock, hints at the possibility of other as yet undiscovered sites further west in Ayrshire.[8] Four phases of occupation have been identified at Loudon Hill, all Flavian in date (late first century AD). This was the first, short-lived Roman invasion and occupation of Scotland, and by AD 110 all Roman troops had withdrawn to the Stanegate frontier (approximately the line of the later Hadrian's Wall). A second invasion followed on the orders of Emperor Antoninus Pius in AD 138, and many earlier forts were reoccupied. As a showpiece, the Antonine Wall, 60 km in length, was constructed along the Forth-Clyde isthmus. Further phases of abandonment and reoccupation ensued, due to pressures elsewhere in the empire, before Hadrian's Wall was re-established as the northernmost frontier in the later second century AD.

The excavation of Loudon Hill produced no detailed evidence for dating of the primary phases. Nevertheless, the possibility that the primary phase of occupation may date to the early Roman penetration into Scotland under Agricola (AD 77–84) must be borne in mind, although at present no fort from this period can be definitely identified further north than Malton in Yorkshire.[9] The isolation of the fort at Loudon Hill is difficult to explain, but its function during part of its life must have been to keep a watchful eye on a section of road identified to the north-west, which probably led to the Ayrshire coast.[10]

Roman finds from Ayrshire are rare. The two coins which have been found, one from Auchinleck and one from in or near Cumnock, are fourth century AD in date, that is, late Roman period. Finds of Roman coins are often interpreted as payment to the local tribes to keep the peace. Neither of these coins is contemporary with the fort at Loudon Hill, and no recognisably native sites are known in the vicinity of Cumnock. Despite the proximity of the two find spots, they should perhaps be seen as stray finds.

Each year, aerial photography and field surveys are revealing new sites of all periods. Further research will almost certainly shed further light on Roman Ayrshire, and lead to a better understanding of the prehistoric period in general.

the early historic and early medieval period

Although west central Scotland contains a number of important settlement and ecclesiastical sites dating to the early historic period, the visible remains are largely limited to a range of carved stone monuments associated with the early church. Govan church, for instance, contains one of the finest but least known collections of Early Christian stones in Scotland—some forty-one in all, dating from *c* AD 900–1200. The most important settlement site in this period was at Dumbarton Rock (NS 400 744), considerably to the north of Cumnock. This dramatic volcanic plug was the principal stronghold of the Strathclyde Britons from at least the fifth century AD. Little now survives of the early historic fortifications or of the *urbs* (town) mentioned by Bede, but excavations in the 1970s revealed the remains of a rampart on the east peak, and exotic finds such as imported Mediterranean pottery and Merovingian glass. Closer to Cumnock, there is little trace of the early historic period in the archaeological record.

The introduction of feudal systems of land tenure during the twelfth and thirteenth centuries was accompanied by the construction of new types of military fortifications, the best known of which are the mottes, or earthwork castle mounds. These vary considerably in size and shape but are often circular 'pudding basin' types. In some case, natural mounds were scarped to form the motte, while in others material for the mound was quarried from a surrounding ditch, itself an integral part of the defences. Neighbouring Clydesdale boasts several examples: that at Abington (NS 932 249) retains an outer bailey; while that at Carnwath (NS 974 466), one of the most impressive Norman earthworks to survive in the area, may have been built for William de Sommerville who came from Yorkshire to Libberton at the invitation of David I, and died in 1160. Near Cumnock, Mote Hill (NS 5755 2069) is the possible site of a motte and bailey castle; while 'Castle Hill' at Borland (NS 5854 1740) is an earthwork mound of unknown date.

The medieval barony of Cumnock was extensive, stretching southwards from the River Lugar to Ayrshire's southern boundary. By the early fourteenth century it was held by the Earls of March,[11] and it passed to a cadet branch of the family—the Dunbars—in 1374–5.[12] The barony was to remain in their hands until the seventeenth century. The seat of the barony was at Cumnock Castle, on the site of present-day New Cumnock. Originally of motte-and-bailey construction, it was a sufficiently substantial residence for it to become the quarters of Edward II during his offensive against Robert Bruce in the 1320s.[13] An alternative name for the castle was Blackcraig.[14] Near the confluence of the Lugar and Glaisnock rivers, 9 km further north, a church or chapel was founded at an unknown date, although certainly before the mid fourteenth century, and, some would argue, before 1300.[15] This became the parish church for the barony, and was in the patronage of the baron of Cumnock. The rectory of Cumnock was appropriated to Glasgow Cathedral,[16] which sustained the parish church with a vicar. A glebe of two merklands of old extent was also provided to support the local priest.[17] There were, therefore, two distinct places with the name Cumnock; this is shown on early maps of the area, such as that of John Adair in 1685 **figure 3**.

12

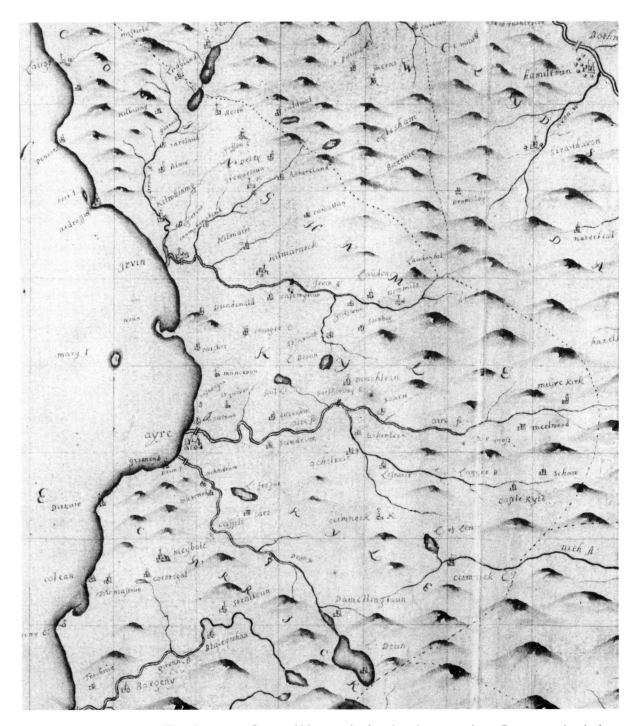

The placename 'Cumnock' has received various interpretations. One suggestion is that it is formed from the two elements 'com', a bosom or hollow, and 'cnoc', a hill. Thus, Cumnock nestles in the bosom of the surrounding hills.[18] It has been argued, however, that this is an unlikely origin, as the compound name is formed with Cymric (Welsh) and Gaelic elements.[19] An alternative explanation is that the word originates from the two generics, 'cumar' meaning 'meeting' and 'oich' meaning 'water'.[20] A third suggested derivation is from the Gaelic 'cam', bent, and 'cnoc', hill—the bent, crooked or sloping hill;[21] a fourth is from the Gaelic 'Cumanag', a little shrine, with possible associations with the church at Cumnock.[22]

the medieval and modern periods

Nothing certain is known of any settlement beside the parish church of Cumnock or the castle further south prior to the granting of burgh status. Both castles and churches, however, offered a measure of protection, if merely psychological; and both would require supplies and services from nearby inhabitants. It is thus probable that there was a clustering of settlement around both of these focal points. Early references to Cumnock, however, do not specify whether they are to settlement beside Cumnock Castle or Cumnock church. A 1313 document, for example, granting the lands of John de Seton to Roger, son of Finlay, in recompense for the stealing of his stud, speaks of a 'tenementum de Comnok' (a tenement in Cumnock).[23] A charter of 1509 also refers to the inhabitants of Cumnock 'present and future', which suggests at least some minimal settlement there already.[24]

On 27 September 1509 James IV created Cumnock, that is the northerly settlement, a burgh of barony.[25] This formed part of a pattern of new burghs in this region of Ayrshire: Newmilns (1491), Auchinleck (1507), Cumnock (1509), Mauchline (1510) and Maybole (1516).[26] The principal desire of the crown in setting up burghs of barony, such as Cumnock, was to favour important subjects, in this case James Dunbar of Cumnock, with a local market.[27] Cumnock was well situated to function as a market centre, being in a strategic position at the junction of the main Ayr to Edinburgh route and the road from Glasgow to Nithsdale and the Borders.

The inhabitants of this new burgh were to have the right to 'buy and sell in the said burgh wine, wax, pitch and bitumen, woollen and linen cloth, both broad and narrow, wool, skins, oxhides, salt, butter, cheese and all other kinds of merchandise, together with power and liberty to possess and keep in the said burgh bakers, braziers, tanners, butchers, sellers of flesh and fish, and all other tradesmen belonging to the liberty of a burgh in barony.' The charter went on to specify that the burgesses and inhabitants were 'to have and maintain, perpetually, a market cross and a market on the Saturday of each week, as well as an annual public fair, with right to uplift dues'.[28]

These were important economic concessions, not only for the superior of the burgh, but also for the local people who by the late sixteenth and early seventeenth centuries included notaries and smiths.[29] How far they actually enjoyed these benefits in the sixteenth century is unclear. So are the details of whether the burgh functioned constitutionally, according to the royal charter, electing bailies and other officers. The Privy Council records of 1575 mentioned the 'clachan' (or village) of Cumnock and the 'said toun of Cumnok' and houses therein,[30] and there were references to the 'clachan' of Cumnock in the *Register of the Great Seal* in 1630, 1638 and 1654.[31] All this suggests that, while there was an established settlement, it was not necessarily functioning as a burgh in the constitutional sense. In 1547, when Patrick Dunbar, son and heir of Alexander Dunbar of Cumnock, was granted the lands and barony of Cumnock, many of the pertinents were listed, such as the manor and the tower, but there was no mention of a burgh.[32] In 1630 and 1662, however, it was referred to specifically as a burgh.[33] Cumnock was not alone in not taking up the full privileges implied in burghal status; Auchinleck, for example, probably never adopted any aspects of its burghal charter.[34]

This impression of Cumnock is reinforced by the lack of burgh court records, which could have been lost, but more probably were never compiled. There is also a telling lack of references to 'burgesses' in the primary sources.[35] Since the inhabitants of the settlement had been granted the right to buy and sell through the market, as indicated in the foundation charter, there would have been little necessity to purchase burgess-ship, which was often a prerequisite to setting up a stall in the market. The routine administration of the town would have been dealt with at the superior's baron court, and the town appears to have been controlled by a bailie nominated by the burgh superior. If this is correct, the burgh superior took up his right to have a market, from which he gained financially through the payment of tolls, but did not bother to establish a constitutional burgh. This would appear to be confirmed to some extent by events in the nineteenth century. In 1833, a Cumnock man, James Crawford, questioned the legality of the Earl of Dumfries, Lord Bute, raising customs, or taxes, on certain goods sold at the town fair. His argument was that the right to raise such dues at the market place of Cumnock had been vested in the magistrates of the burgh by the charter of 1509. A court case, however, found for Lord Bute,[36] largely on the evidence of the 1681 act of parliament that granted the dues from the weekly market and three fairs to the baron of Cumnock, thereby, in effect, rescinding the original burghal charter.[37]

14

figure 4
The market cross

Markets were still held in Cumnock in the early seventeenth century,[38] although there is no mention of a tolbooth. The tolbooth was, for most burghs, the most important secular building, a key symbol of burgh status; it was here that the market dues were collected, the burgh council and court held their meetings and, often, the town jail was housed. But Cumnock seems not to have had such a building. In 1688, when the local minister, the Reverend David Houston, was in custody, prior to being taken to Edinburgh by government dragoons, he was warded in the Blue Tower Inn in Cumnock.[39] This, too, suggests that Cumnock did not have a tolbooth.

The market, in any burgh, usually clustered around or near the cross, which for Cumnock probably functioned also as the collection point for market dues **figure 4**. Wooden forebuildings jutting from the dwellings lining the market street, and free-standing booths or stalls, displayed the goods for sale. These would be the locally produced or finished manufactories of the town's craftsmen and produce from the surrounding countryside, as well as basics such as bread, meat and ale. By the end of the seventeenth century Cumnock had several resident merchants and craftsmen. The latter included weavers, tailors, dyers, coopers, baxters (bakers), cordiners (leather workers), masons, tanners, smiths and a glover.[40] Merchants from other towns also visited Cumnock. In 1600, two traders arrived at the town, having been forbidden entry into Ayr, for fear of plague. Whether they were carriers or not, plague broke out with such virulence that the town burial ground—the square around the church—could not accommodate the dead. A mass burial site was established at Greenbraehead, along Glaisnock Street.[41]

It has been traditionally said in Cumnock that the first site of the market cross was at the top of Townhead, or High Street as it was sometimes called, 'where the street is narrowest and slopes down towards the old ironstone pit' **figure 5**.[42] Such a siting would not only have been unusual but also unlikely. It would have been quite exceptional to place an urban market cross at the outskirts of settlement. A likelier site is further west, in Townhead, but nearer to the parish church and the 'merchant shops' to the south of the kirkyard (*see* **gazetteer** entry for the market cross; pp 51–2).[43]

figure 5
Townhead Street

Cumnock had also received the right in its burghal charter to hold annual fairs.[44] In 1681 this was extended to three fairs per year, as well as the weekly market.[45] These occasions would attract traders from further afield, as well as the residents of Cumnock's rural hinterland, and would need a large open space. The original site was near Stepends Ford, in the north-west of the town, but gradually this area became developed. By the middle of the eighteenth century a bridge had been built beside the ford and a tanyard and kiln occupied part of the traditional site of the fair.[46] The fair had to be held elsewhere but it is uncertain where its site was transferred to. One probable site is at the east end of Townhead where settlement did not encroach on open space. If this is correct, it is possible that the present-day marker in the road at Townhead alludes not to the site of the market cross, as traditionally claimed, but to the later site of the fair.

A traditional eighteenth- and nineteenth-century accompaniment to the spring fair was the horse race. This may have been an institution of some antiquity, for it is known that as early as 1610 a quarrel broke out on the 'occasioun of ane horse race whiche was run at Cumnoke'.[47]

The parish church was an important focal point of the town's life **figure 17**. Set in the centre of the town, it dominated the surrounding dwellings. The close links of town and church were formed as early as the burghal charter, when it was specified that the glebe lands should be alienated and divided up into burgage plots for the potential new inhabitants.[48] It is, therefore, probable that the first urban settlement was close to the church. In the early seventeenth century, the barony of Cumnock, along with the patronage of the church, was sold by the Dunbars. It passed through a number of hands, ultimately coming into the possession of the Crichtons, Lords Sanquhar, who in 1633 were promoted in the peerage as Earls of Dumfries.[49] One of their number, Charles, Lord Crichton, was created a lord of regality in 1680; consequently, Cumnock, as a burgh of barony, assumed the title of a burgh of regality which meant that it functioned very much with the privileges of a royal burgh, although not subject to the king. A decision made in 1650 that the extensive parish of Old Cumnock should be bisected was temporarily annulled in 1667 after pressure from the Earl of Dumfries, the annulment being confirmed by act of parliament in 1681; but this was not to last and in 1691 the separation of the parish was confirmed.[50]

Attachment to their faith was to bring a number of Cumnock residents into conflict with the authorities in the two decades after the Restoration of 1660. In 1662 the parish minister, John Cunningham, was deprived of his charge for failure to conform to the episcopal rule reintroduced in the reign of Charles II. He was replaced by ministers appointed by the Earl of Dumfries, but the new incumbents were not always favourably received by the parishioners. Patrick Crawford from Cumnock, for example, was fined the swingeing sum of £2,000 Scots for refusing to conform in 1662.

The hard core of the Covenanting movement was the radical south-west of Scotland. A number of Cumnock men were involved in the Pentland Rising—the Covenanting march from Dumfries via Mauchline, Ochiltree and Cumnock to the débâcle of the battle of Rullion Green in 1666. This was followed by repression, and two local men were amongst those who paid for insurrection. Patrick McNaught was indicted in 1667, and George Crawford, a Cumnock weaver, was executed in December 1666. Unrest in 1678 brought a billeting of some of the Highland Host in the parish. An armed uprising followed, which ended disastrously with the Covenanters' defeat at the battle of Bothwell Brig. Two Cumnock men, John Gemill and James Mirrie, were taken prisoner, incarcerated in the Greyfriars Kirk in Edinburgh, sentenced to transportation to the American colonies and drowned—with many others—when their prison ship, *The Crown of London*, went down off the coast of Orkney.

Opposition to episcopacy continued, however. In 1682, the Earl of Dumfries undertook to examine all the parishioners of Cumnock and fine those whose children had been baptised by non-conformist ministers. The following year, a court was set up in Cumnock to ensure regular attendance at church. The year 1684 saw stronger measures introduced, in an attempt to force offenders to take the Test Oath of loyalty. Cumnock men featured in the proclamation of outlaws to be apprehended: Alexander Stillie, John Campbell and William Campbell from Townhead of Cumnock, James Dalziel from near the kirk of Cumnock, Robert McGavin and John Weir, a tailor, from Cumnock. In 1685 and 1686, Robert Mitchell of Cumnock was shot, and a number of Covenanters were brought to the town for execution and buried on Gallows Hill. The body of the celebrated Covenanting preacher Reverend Alexander Peden was even exhumed and brought to Cumnock to be ritually hanged (although this seems not to have been carried out) and buried at the foot of the gallows. The news of the accession of William and Mary in 1689 and the formal establishment of Presbyterianism in Scotland in 1690 must have been received with relief. The reaction in Cumnock probably speaks for itself. Ninety armed men cornered the Episcopalian minister in the churchyard, tore his clothing and ejected him from the town with the warning not to preach there again.[51]

The available evidence suggests that Cumnock was a small but well-established community by the seventeenth century. The objection, in 1622, of Cumnock residents to the attempts of the burgh superior to bring in skilled workers from outside the town implies that, in the eyes of the locals at least, the home workforce was adequate both in numbers and ability.[52] The town must by this time have possessed at least a few streets and a fair number of houses. By 1594 the town had a resident notary.[53] A school had been established before 1625 when Helen Lockhart endowed it with £20 in her will.[54]

A wider picture of the topography of the town before the mid eighteenth century is, however, difficult to draw. There is little doubt that settlement, while extending out along Townhead, also continued to cluster near the church, but whether the dwellings nearby faced towards the graveyard surrounding the church, as suggested by some, or were orientated away from the graveyard, is unclear.[55] It is possible that the merchant dwellings on the south side of the graveyard faced on to a thoroughfare, called Back Street in the nineteenth century and later Tower Street, which was in effect a continuation of Townhead Street. There would have been little virtue in having the main doors to the houses entering and exiting into a graveyard. The same was in all probability true of the properties on the east side of the graveyard; the placing of the market cross in the north-east corner of the erstwhile churchyard or graveyard, sometime before 1769, might suggest that there was no thoroughfare here at this date, if the hypothesis that the cross was moved out of Townhead Street to ease congestion is correct **figure 6**.[56] The precise orientation of these properties cannot, however, be certain until the exact line of the path north to the manse is established. Likewise the properties to the west of the churchyard may have fronted a later street, named Back Vennel, rather than the churchyard itself.

By the mid eighteenth century, a clearer view of Cumnock emerges. Cartographic evidence indicates that the town still focused on, and around, the church and graveyard and Townhead Street **figure 10**.[57] Four main arteries linked the town with the surrounding

figure 6
A corner of
the Square

hinterland: the Auchinleck road entered from the north-west, crossing the Lugar by Stepends ford; the Muirkirk road passed by Barrhill and the gallows, arriving at the north-east corner of the churchyard; from the south-west, the road from Ayr entered Cumnock after crossing the Glaisnock Water at Dubb Ford, passing along the Townfoot, or an extension to the later-named Tower Street where there is evidence of settlement; and the route to and from New Cumnock passed eastwards along High Street or Townhead Street.

The later eighteenth century was to see some changes to this basic street pattern, as a result of the Ayrshire Turnpike Acts of 1766 and 1774 which introduced payment for the use of roads, at turnpikes (or gates), and the improvements to parish roads effected by the Earl of Dumfries. In 1753 a bridge was constructed across the Lugar at Stepend, although not without mishap. The *Gentleman's Magazine* of August 1753 recorded:

This county having some time ago contracted with an undertaker to build a bridge over the Lugar at Cumnock, the work was so far advanced that on Tuesday, the 7th ult., one arch was finished and the timber frame removed, but this afternoon, when all the hands were at work, the arch fell down at once, by which eight persons were killed on the spot and four more much bruised.[58]

It appears that until this time the route to Townhead Street passed from Stepends Ford in a dog-leg southwards to the west of the graveyard and the church, which had been rebuilt in 1754 (*see* p 28), and then turned east along the later-named Tower Street to join Townhead Street. A more direct route was blocked by the churchyard. It was therefore decided to abandon the traditional burial ground for a site along Barrhill Road, beside the gallows. A route was then forced along the north and east edges of the superseded churchyard and, with a difficult exit from this new square, it entered Townhead Street.[59] It was around this time that the market cross was moved to the north-east corner of the Square, from where it was again removed, to ease congestion, to its present site south of the church. A further radical change came sometime before 1775, when a bridge was built across the Glaisnock, just south of the Square, thus permitting a more direct access to New Cumnock via Glaisnock Street, with a new road to Ayr branching off westwards **figure 7**.

This new street pattern—which is still reflected in the current road system—was to bring significant change to Cumnock and its townspeople. Wheeled traffic had not been common at the beginning of the eighteenth century and Ayrshire farmers found sledges more suitable. By the 1790s there were five wheeled carriages and 150 carts in the parish of Old Cumnock. Much of this traffic passed through Cumnock, strategically placed as it was on a long-established crossroads. By 1787, stage coaches also passed through Cumnock on their way from Glasgow, through Kilmarnock, to Carlisle. For the welfare of

18

figure 7

The bridge over
the Glaisnock

travellers, the New Inn, later called the Dumfries Arms Hotel, was established on Glaisnock Street.[60] It was here that Walter Scott stayed on a visit to the town. He was later to recall that Cumnock was 'where beds are as hard as a plank'.[61] The Armstrongs' 1775 map of Ayrshire, while not totally accurate, does reveal the importance of the New Inn in the Cumnock locality **figure 8**.[62]

Cumnock maintained closest contact, not surprisingly, with the network of small towns in its locality. A number of its residents were known to Robert Burns: William Simson, the local schoolmaster from 1788 to 1815, was immortalised as 'Winsome Willie'; John Kennedy, the factor to the Earl of Dumfries, corresponded with Burns; and the Secession minister, James Hall, may also have known him; and Annie Rankine, the inspiration of 'Corn Rigs', married a Cumnock man and stayed in the town as 'Mrs Merry' until her death in 1843.[63]

The population of Cumnock increased during the latter part of the eighteenth century. According to the *Statistical Account* (drawn up in the 1790s), there were 580 residents in 1765 and by 1792 this figure had risen to 787.[64] A number of occupations were available locally to these townspeople, including weaving, shoemaking, tanning and dyeing.[65] Presumably most of the tanning took place at the Tanyard, close by the Lugar, which offered a ready supply of water and was also an accessible disposal dump. There were thirty-three shoemakers, who manufactured a variety of leather goods, one tanner and two skin and wool dealers. Textile manufacturing, however, was the principal craft by the late eighteenth century: thirty-five handlooms producing traditional coarse linen and woollen materials were supplemented by thirty-nine new handlooms for cotton and muslins. This involved twenty-eight weavers and their apprentices. A further seven were stocking weavers; and three lint dressers, two walkers and fifteen tailors were involved in the finishing processes. To encourage the weaving industry Lady Dumfries established the 'Jeannie House' in Lugar Steet, which housed looms for the use of local people (*see* p 21).[66]

From the early 1760s efforts were made by the fifth Earl of Dumfries and his successors to boost the local economy. Their main residence was Dumfries House, a little to the west of Cumnock on the banks of the Lugar (*see* p 45). From here, a concerted investment was made, particularly in the exploitation of local minerals. Coal had been discovered in the area as early as 1745.[67] Coal-mining, begun at nearby Garlaff in 1768, was potentially profitable given its essential part in the production of lime, which was increasingly in demand for agricultural improvements. The opening of further mines in Coalburn and, temporarily, near Pluckburn, at Auchingilsie and near Grimgrew, did not meet with the anticipated success. In spite of the appointment in 1790 of James Taylor, a medically trained local man with considerable knowledge of the steam engine, the expected boom did not materialise and in 1792 there were only eighteen colliers in the entire parish.[68]

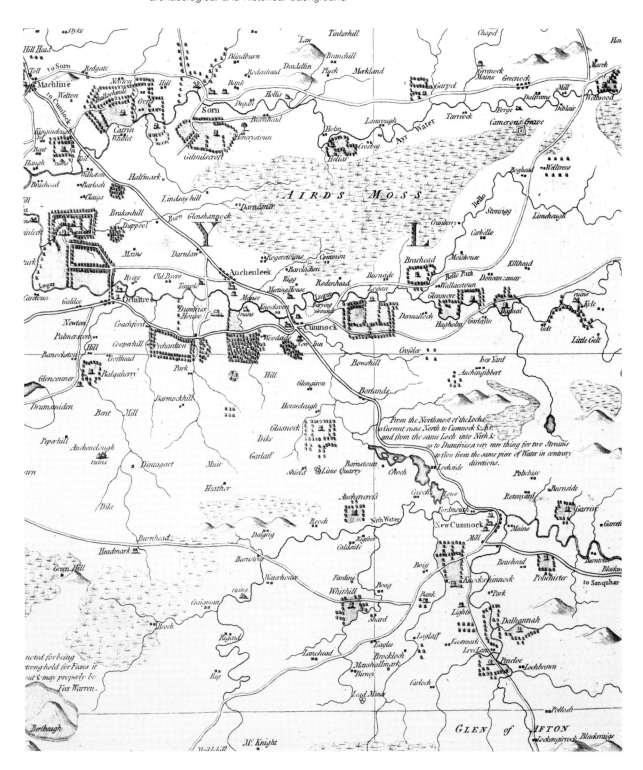

figure 8

The Armstrongs' map,
1755 *National Library
of Scotland*

A rare mineral, graphite, discovered at Craigman near Cumnock, was mined from 1770 onwards. This led to a further manufacturing process in Cumnock—pottery. Graphite, blended with fireclay, was an important component in the manufacture of refractory crucibles. A couple of ventures into pottery manufacture in the 1780s had failed. Lady Dumfries, however, had taken an interest in pottery techniques and processes, and became aware of the potential benefits to the local community of the establishment of a new pottery in Cumnock, particularly if under the management of James Taylor. The Cumnock area could supply all the raw materials: fireclay for the kilns, coals to heat them, quality clay suitable for brown-glazed domestic ware and, from the Dumfries estate, white-burning porcelainous clay for more prestigious ware. In 1792 three potters were brought from Glasgow to man the works under the supervision of Taylor. Lady Dumfries also loaned £500 to the venture. Overall, unfortunately, the pottery venture was a failure—partly because an attempt was made to produce differing types of wares which were fired

20

figure 9
William Roy's military
survey, 1747–55
(maps C949)
British Library

at different temperatures in the kilns, but also possibly because of the inexperience of the Glasgow potters in fields other than crucibles and coarseware pottery. Pantile making, promoted by Taylor, and fine ware were never truly profitable; ultimately the pottery became a small producer, using the local clays, of cheap country brownware.[69]

This was not the end of the line for graphite, as it was also used in manufacturing pencils. Although Cumnock pencils were rudimentary, pencil-making as a whole was in its infancy. Manufactured under Taylor's supervision, they continued to be produced on a limited scale in Cumnock until the 1840s; the market for them extended as far as London.[70]

Population expansion accelerated in the nineteenth century. The 787 inhabitants of 1792 had more than doubled to 1,600 by 1831, and probably reached 2,600 by the 1860s.[71] Much of the reason for this expansion was the growth of local trades and opportunities for employment. Most significant was still the weaving craft. By 1811 there were seventy muslin weavers and by the 1830s more than 120 looms in the town. Most of this was concentrated in the Townhead region, where virtually every house had at least one cotton loom; six had four looms and three had six. The town also housed several agents of Glasgow firms, who marketed the cotton cloth. The boom times were to end for cotton hand-loom weaving, however, in the 1840s and 1850s, with the introduction of power looms and the scarcity of raw cotton during the American Civil War.[72] Despite the introduction of new industries, this brought much distress to the weaving population; by 1889 only one weaver remained in Townhead, along with another two in other parts of the town.[73]

Mineral extraction and the potteries continued in the nineteenth century on a moderate scale. A new manufacture, however, was the making of snuff boxes, which reached its heyday between 1820 and 1830, when over a hundred people were employed. Whether the 'invisible wooden hinge', which added to the value of the boxes, was a Cumnock invention or a secret imported from Auchinleck is not certain.[74] Decorated boxes could command prices as high as £7; scene-painters could earn two guineas a week, box-makers half that sum and varnishers twelve shillings. By 1843, with snuff-taking becoming less popular, the six box-manufacturing businesses had dwindled to three. An important market was the passing coach trade, but after 1850, with the arrival of the railway in Cumnock, stage coaches were phased out. By the 1880s the snuff box industry had disappeared from the town.[75]

Cumnock continued to remain a centre for local marketing; indeed, this function may have increased in the nineteenth century. Although the *Old Statistical Account* indicates that the weekly markets, authorised in 1509, were no longer held at the end of the eighteenth century,[76] locals still recognised Thursdays as 'market day'.[77] Retail shops, banks and an improving communications network, begun by the stage coach and completed by the arrival of the railway, to some extent superseded the old market system, although fairs remained a vital part of Cumnock life. The records contain evidence that three fairs were held in 1813 and 1830; there were four a few years later and, for a while, a fifth was held.[78] One of the main functions of these fairs was to provide a venue for the sale of local agricultural produce and livestock, but equally important was their role as feeing fairs— the occasion when farm labourers were hired **figure 10**. While Cumnock may have been making sterling efforts to develop its own manufactory industries, it was still in the mid nineteenth century, as it had been from the sixteenth century, a market centre that relied on the support of its rural neighbours.

There were signs, however, that Cumnock was ceasing to be a small town with close contacts solely with its near neighbours. Religious differences saw a proliferation of impressive new church buildings (*see* pp 43–4); improvements in school facilities resulted not merely in better buildings (*see* p 30), but also, according to the *New Statistical Account* in 1837, there were 'very few above the age of fourteen who [were] not able to read and write, as parents evince[d] a laudable anxiety to give their children the common branches of education';[79] and the arrival of the railways would bring a radical reorientation to the thinking of the people of Cumnock. The town morphology, as can be seen on the

figure 10
The Feeing Fair,
the Square

figure 11
Glaisnock Street,
with triumphal arch

nineteenth-century Ordnance Survey maps, responded. The basic street pattern remained, with the old town clustered around it, but, spreading out from this focal point, the main arteries reflected the growth that had taken place. Townhead Street, with its cotton weavers, was fully developed, still retaining small, thatched cottages, shown in nineteenth-century photographs; Glaisnock Street was built up on the west side as far as the Dumfries Arms; on the east side, behind Greenbraehead, was a smithy and, beyond, a new gas works and the potteries **figure 11**; Ayr Road, leading off Glaisnock Street, was built up on the west side, where the new Free Church stood (*see* **figure 12** *and* p 44); Barrhill, leading to three coal and ironstone pits, was still largely open road; and across the Stepends Bridge, along the Auchinleck Road, a number of substantial villas had been erected (*see* p 42).

Radical changes were to come in the later nineteenth century. In 1866 Cumnock became a police burgh. The new council was to institute many environmental improvements, essential for a community in the process of changing from a small market town to a coal-mining centre.[80] The changes that this was to bring both to the fabric of and attitudes in the town, and the impact of Cumnock's famous resident Keir Hardie,

figure 12
Ayr Road

founder of the Labour Party, have been fully explored in John Strawhorn's *New History of Cumnock*. The twentieth century, and the decline of coal-mining in the area, was to witness, yet again, a sometimes painful transformation to a Cumnock that still maintains some industry and functions as a market centre,[81] but is now essentially a dormitory town for nearby larger conurbations.

notes

1   A Morrison & I Hughes, *The Stone Ages in Ayrshire* (Ayrshire Archaeological and Natural History Society, 1989), 15.

2   T Darvill, *Prehistoric Britain* (London, 1987), 63–4.

3   *Ibid*, 75.

4   A Morrison, *The Bronze Age in Ayrshire* (Ayrshire Archaeological and Natural History Society, Ayrshire Collection, xii, no 4, 1978), 143–7.

5   Darvill, *Prehistoric Britain*, 103.

6   *Ibid*, 133.

7   R Feachem, *Guide to Prehistoric Scotland* (London, 1978), 110.

8   W Hanson & G Maxwell, *Rome's North West Frontier* (Edinburgh, 1983), 41.

9   *Ibid*, 35.

10   *Ibid*, 71.

11   J Strawhorn, *The New History of Cumnock* (Cumnock, 1966), 16.

12   *RMS*, i, no 291; *NSA*, v, 479.

13   *CDS*, iii, nos 5–7, 497, 503; H Lorimer, *A Corner of Old Strathclyde* (Glasgow, 1952), 45.

14   As noted, for example, on the Armstrongs' map of Ayrshire, 1755; and on the map 'Scottish Castles' (n d).

15   Androw of Wyntoun, *The Orygynale Cronykil of Scotland*, ed. D. Laing (Edinburgh, 1872), ii, 487; J Warrick, *The History of Old Cumnock* (London, 1899), 63.

16   *Registrum Episcopatus Glasguensis*, ed C Innes (2 vols, Maitland Club, 1843), i, lxiv.

17   *RMS*, vi, no 2045.

18   *NSA*, v, 475.

19   Warrick, *Old Cumnock*, 5.

20   F H Groome, *Ordnance Gazetteer of Scotland: A Survey of Scottish Topography* (6 vols, Edinburgh, 1886), ii, 327.

21   Warrick, *Old Cumnock*, 6.

22   D Love, *A Pictorial History of Cumnock* (Darvel, 1992), 7.

23   *RMS*, ii, no 3376.

24   *RRS*, v, no 38.

25   *Ibid*.

26   G S Pryde, *The Burghs of Scotland: a Critical List* (Glasgow, 1965), 53, 56, 57.

27   *RRS*, v, no 38.

28   *Ibid*.

29   *RPC*, v, 615, 630; vii, 622; viii, 412.

30   *RPC*, ii, 502.

31   *RMS*, viii, no 1563; ix, no 791; x, no 329.

32   *RMS*, iv, no 113.

24

33 *RMS*, viii, no 1563; x, no 339.

34 Strawhorn, *New History*, 19.

35 Records in NLS, RCAHMS and SRO have been fully assessed. Access to papers in Dumfries House, an important source for this Survey, was not granted. John Strawhorn worked extensively on this material in the 1960s. Information from his assessment of the Dumfries House papers has, therefore, been included.

36 Warrick, *Old Cumnock*, 306–7.

37 *APS*, iii, 444–5.

38 *RPC*, vii, 290.

39 Strawhorn, *New History*, 29.

40 *Ibid*, 34.

41 H J Steven, *The Cumnocks Old and New: their History and Associations* (Kilmarnock, 1899), 9.

42 Warrick, *Old Cumnock*, 303.

43 Strawhorn, *New History*, 33.

44 *RMS*, ii. no 3376.

45 *APS*, viii, 444–5.

46 Strawhorn, *New History*, 32–3.

47 *RPC*, ix, 91.

48 *RMS*, ii, no 3376.

49 Strawhorn, *New Cumnock*, 26.

50 *APS*, viii, 338; Warrick, *Old Cumnock*, 2.

51 Strawhorn, *New History*, 27–30.

52 Warrick, *Old Cumnock*, 258.

53 *RPC*, v, 615.

54 Warrick, *Old Cumnock*, 259.

55 Steven, *The Cumnocks*, 10.

56 Strawhorn, *New History*, 39.

57 W Roy, 'Military Survey of Scotland' (1747–1755), sheet 4/5. This is confirmed by the work of Strawhorn on the Dumfries House papers (Strawhorn, *New History*, 49).

58 *Gentleman's Magazine*, August 1753, quoted in Stevens, *The Cumnocks*, 11.

59 Anon, *An Illustrated Guide to Cumnock* (Cumnock Town Council, n d), 9.

60 Much of the information pertinent to the topography of the town is based on the work of Strawhorn who had access to documentation at Dumfries House.

61 J Strawhorn & K Andrew, *Discovering Ayrshire* (Edinburgh, 1988), 176; Stevens, *The Cumnocks*, 13.

62 J Strawhorn, 'An introduction to Armstrongs' map', *Ayrshire Archaeological and Natural History Society Journal* (1959), 235.

63 Strawhorn, *New History*, 50–1.

64 *OSA*, vi, 112.

65 *Ibid*, 119.

66 Strawhorn, *New History*, 40.

67 G Quail, *The Cumnock Potters* (Ayrshire Archaeological and Natural History Society, Ayrshire Monographs, no 12, 1993), 9.

68 Strawhorn, *New History*, 45.

69 Quail, *Cumnock Potters*, 14–18.

70 *Ibid*, 15.

71 Warrick, *Old Cumnock*, 251.

72 Strawhorn, *New History*, 52.

73 *Ibid*, 52–3.

74 Stevens, *The Cumnocks*, 12.

75 *Ibid*, 53–4.

76 *OSA*, vi, 113.

77 Strawhorn, *New History*, 72.

78 *Ibid*.

79 *NSA*, v, 489.

80 J T Cree, 'Here and there: a directory of towns and villages, Cumnock' in J Moore (ed), *Among Thy Green Braes* (Cumnock, 1977), 62–3.

81 I M Dick *et al*, *The Cumnock Area* (London, 1975), 18; J C M Laurenson, *Cumnock and New Cumnock in Old Picture Postcards* (Cumnock, 1983), unpaginated.

area by area assessment

pp 27–39

historic buildings

pp 41–5

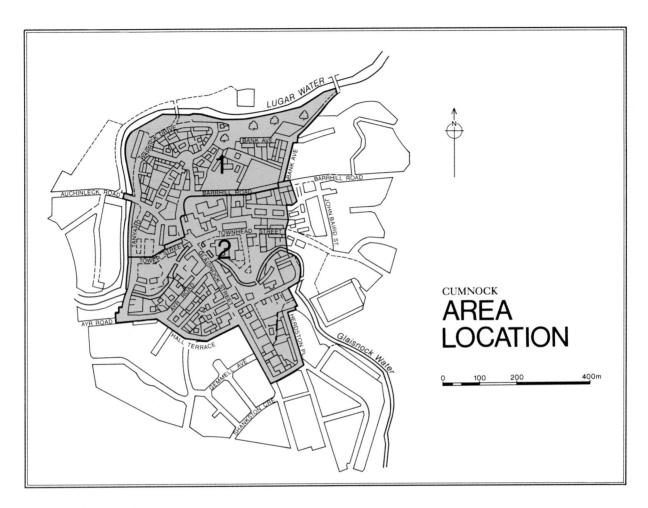

figure 13

Area location map

The medieval core of the town has been divided into two discrete areas **figure 13**: one to the north of the town including the Square (Area 1), and one to the south (Area 2).

The Lugar Water to the north and west, and the Glaisnock Water to the south, provide easily recognisable limits to the development of the medieval town. To a large extent, these natural boundaries have also defined the limits of the study area in this survey. The eastern boundary of the medieval burgh is less easily discerned, and has here been taken to be the west side of John Baird Street.

For reference, areas within areas, ie groups of properties which are bounded on all sides by major streets, have been defined as 'blocks' in the text.

area 1
Lugar Water / Tanyard / the Square / Hamilton Place / Barrhill Road **figure 14**

description

The north side of Tower Street has been extensively landscaped and is now the site of the bus station. This encompasses much of the area between Bank Lane and the Tanyard, and there are two new buildings on or near the Tanyard frontage: the Post Office depot and a block of public toilets. The road itself (the Tanyard) has also been significantly widened to improve traffic flow around the outskirts of the town. The Lugar Water lies immediately to the west of the Tanyard.

At the eastern end of Area 1 is the Square **A**. The parish church **B**, built in 1867, still dominates the Square, and the area around it, once the graveyard, has now been pedestrianised. The market cross **C** now stands at the south-western corner of the Square.

The row of buildings along Bank Lane, to the west of the parish church, face the Square. However, prior to remodelling of the area in the mid eighteenth century, these buildings originally *backed* onto the Square, with their façades on Bank Lane. These façades have largely gone, disguised by the many small additions and extensions to what is now the rear of the properties.

Between Bank Lane and the western end of Lugar Street is a block of buildings, the most notable being the museum. Attached to the north-west corner of the museum is a dilapidated building that is presently boarded up **D**. This in turn is attached to the rear of one of a group of properties that front onto Lugar Street, which includes the Post Office.

On the north side of the Square, directly opposite the parish church (on the corner of Hamilton Place and Lugar Street), are some vacant properties **E**. From here, northwards to beyond Barrhill Road, is a block of mainly old industrial buildings and garages, with areas of waste ground and car parking. Many of these buildings are either vacant or falling into disrepair.

To the west of this block, there are two modern, but temporary-looking buildings: a clinic and a surgery with associated car parking. Three properties that front onto Lugar Street, two to the west of Millbank and one to the east (nos 12–18 Lugar Street), are currently vacant **F**. Two large gardens **G**, perhaps the only burgage plots left in Cumnock, extend from these properties, northwards up the hill. From the rear, nos 16–18 Lugar Street can clearly be seen to have been terraced into the slope. A number of outbuildings and foundations of outbuildings, all dilapidated, can be seen in the back gardens.

To the north of these gardens, and to the west of Millbank, is a large area of open grass around which are set rows of cottages to the north and west. Further west, the ground falls away sharply down to the Lugar Water.

From the corner of Hamilton Place and Barrhill Road, the road climbs steeply up the hill. On the north side of Barrhill Road lies the Old Council Offices, now a school, with some grass and tree areas bordering the road itself. Further up the hill is the graveyard, with the Covenanters' graves **H** by the roadside.

historical background

This area includes the focal point of medieval Cumnock—the parish church **B**. A church or chapel has stood on this site since at least the mid fourteenth century, and possibly from the thirteenth.[1] As the parish church for the barony of Cumnock, it was in the patronage of the feudal superior, and the rectory was appropriated to the cathedral of Glasgow.[2] The present church was built in 1866 as a replacement to one erected in 1754. This latter was a single-storeyed building, with an external staircase to the roof area and a square tower **figure 16**. Attached to it were the jougs, where offenders were placed for public humiliation. When this church was demolished the bell was removed and temporarily hung in a tree in the Strand **figure 20**. It remained here for eight years, being rung twice a day and for worship on Sundays. A new bell was then donated to the church and the old bell was put to service at the public school. Nothing is known of the design of the predecessors to the 1754 church.

Surrounding the church was the kirkyard, which also functioned as the burial ground until it was cleared to permit access to traffic in the mid eighteenth century, thus forming the Square **B**. A glebe of two merklands, provided to support the vicar, stretched northwards and westwards from the kirkyard. The manse stood some distance from the church, near the Lugar Water **I**. The eighteenth-century manse still stands (*see* p 43), although greatly transformed by recent renovations and additions. Not only was the church the spiritual centre of Cumnock parish, it also became the nucleus for the burgh created in 1509, as it was laid down in the charter of burghal erection that the glebe lands should be alienated and laid out in burgage plots on which the inhabitants would build their homes.[3]

It is safe to assume that settlement in the sixteenth century clustered around this point. In all probability, however, the first dwellings around the kirkyard faced away from it, with their frontages onto access vennels, such as Bank Lane, or Vennel, to the west, as indicated above (*see* pp 16).

To the west of Bank Lane stood a large open space, which by the eighteenth century had become known as the Tanyard **J**, a name retained by the modern thoroughfare. This was so called because of the tanning works on this site, which was an ideal one, being beside a ready supply of water. The Lugar could also function as a refuse tip for noxious waste associated with the tanning process.

archaeological potential and future development

The draft Local Plan of 1994 proposes a number of environmental improvements for this area, as part of its Town Action Plan, including:

i   the construction of a new link road between Barrhill Road and the Tanyard;
ii   the prohibition of access from the Square to Glaisnock Street and the provision of additional parking in the area; and
iii increased pedestrianisation of Lugar Street.

A number of gap sites are considered ripe for redevelopment, but none is referred to specifically. Further improvements to the appearance of the central area of the town are also anticipated.

As well as its Conservation Area status, with sixteen listed buildings, the Square must be seen as an archaeologically sensitive area of primary importance within the burgh. This is the site of the early medieval church and associated graveyard, of which little is known. The extent to which the underlying archaeological material has been damaged by improvements from the mid eighteenth century onwards is difficult to assess at this stage, in the absence of any previous archaeological work. Although development here is unlikely

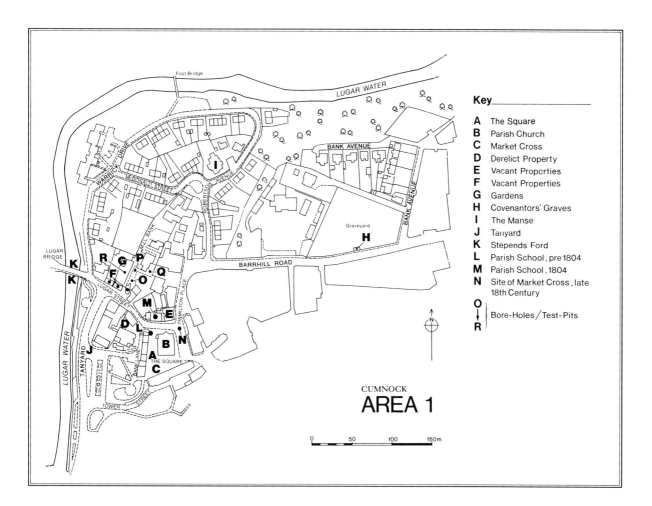

Key

A The Square
B Parish Church
C Market Cross
D Derelict Property
E Vacant Properties
F Vacant Properties
G Gardens
H Covenantors' Graves
I The Manse
J Tanyard
K Stepends Ford
L Parish School, pre 1804
M Parish School, 1804
N Site of Market Cross, late 18th Century
O
⊢ } Bore-Holes / Test-Pits
R

CUMNOCK
AREA 1

0   50   100   150m

figure 14

Area 1

history

Prior to becoming a tanning yard, part of this land and that further north, on the other side of the path leading to Stepends Ford **K**, had served as the site of the fair. The burghal charter had granted the right to an annual fair, and this was extended in 1681 to three a year.[4] Such occasions would attract not only Cumnock residents and their neighbours from the surrounding rural hinterland, but also traders from further afield. In the eighteenth and nineteenth centuries, a traditional accompaniment to the spring fair was the horse race. How early this event had begun in Cumnock is unclear, but it may

archaeology

in the foreseeable future, any further environmental improvements must be archaeologically assessed.

The frontages, both around the Square **A** and of the major streets within the historic core of the town, must also remain a priority; sealed below the foundations, remains of the very earliest settlement in the burgh may survive, in the form of timber buildings. A cellar study was beyond the scope of this survey but, particularly along the main street frontages, approximately half the properties would be expected to have cellars; cellared properties are less likely to have archaeological remains preserved beneath them.

Other than the historic standing buildings, there is little physical evidence in the form of existing property boundaries, to indicate the layout of the medieval burgage plots in this part of the town. Cartographic evidence indicates that the burgh was a patchwork of small gardens or burgage plots, but, sadly, almost none survive today. The only remaining burgage plots appear to be two behind the Lugar Street frontage (north side). Here **G**, evidence may survive of medieval garden soils, rubbish pits or middens, all of which would provide evidence for the date and nature of earlier land use. Areas of waste ground elsewhere behind the Lugar Street frontage may yield similar information. Given the proposed link-up of Barrhill Road and Lugar Street, the archaeology of this area, the backlands and frontage, is under immediate threat and will need to be monitored and recorded during construction works.

have been of some antiquity, as there is reference to a horse race run in the town in 1610.[5]

Development in this area of the town in the mid eighteenth century—the building of the tanyard and a kiln and the construction of a bridge beside the ford—meant that the fair had to be moved to another part of the town (*see* p 15). Annual feeing fairs, when labourers were taken on by local farmers, continued to be held here **figure 10**.

The purpose of the Lugar Bridge was to facilitate the entry of wheeled traffic into Cumnock. Until the mid eighteenth century, traffic had dog-legged southwards down the Back Vennel after crossing the Lugar. A decision to open up the kirkyard to traffic meant a change of site for the town burial yard and the removal of the graves and burial monuments; the north and east sides of what is now the Square became roadways.

The parish school was by this time sited at the north-west corner of the Square **L**. Where the first school was sited is unclear, but it was probably also near to the parish church. Cumnock had a school as early as 1625, when Helen Lockhart endowed it with £20 in her will.[6] In 1804, the school was relocated, but still in the Square, to the site of the present Clydesdale Bank **M**. It subsequently transferred to Barrhill Road.

Also in the Square, at the north-east corner, was the market cross **N**. When it was first placed here is unclear, but it was there before 1769[7] and possibly was erected soon after the kirkyard ceased to function as a burial ground. The cross is still extant **C**, now placed to the south of the parish church where it does not impede traffic **figure 4**. An inscription on the cross, '1703 repaired 1778', suggests that it had been in existence prior to being located in the Square (*see* pp 51–2). Cumnock had been granted the right to a weekly market in its burghal charter, and it is clear that markets were still being held in the early seventeenth

history

archaeology

The area to the west of the Square, between Tower Street and Lugar Street, has seen redevelopment and landscaping in recent years. This was the area where the tanning industry was concentrated. The impact of recent landscaping on the survival of any industrial archaeology here is difficult to assess, but the remains of tanning pits or tanks, often sunk deep into the ground, must be expected to survive.

Street improvements, such as those proposed for Lugar Street, may reveal features sealed beneath the modern road surface. These could take the form of earlier street levels or wells, or even features which predate the construction of the street itself. Any street improvements, therefore, must also be archaeologically monitored.

As a footnote to this area, an environmental improvement scheme has been proposed for the Mote Hill, subject to the District Council acquiring the area as an extension to Woodroad Park. Although it is outside the study area, this proposed improvement scheme is also very likely to have archaeological implications as this may be the site of an early earthwork castle.

bore-hole surveys and other features

No archaeological work has previously been carried out in this area, nor have there been any archaeological chance finds. Engineers' bore-holes, however, can offer a tantalising glimpse of the nature and depth of underground deposits. In advance of the proposal to re-route Barrhill Road to join up with the Tanyard at Lugar Bridge, one such bore-hole survey has been carried out on the line of the new roadway. Four test-pits were examined **figure 14**:

O

A depth of approximately 0.20 m of very mixed topsoil was revealed, overlying 0.15–0.20 m of weathered natural subsoil.

century.[8] They had died out, probably because of the growing number of retail shops, by the late eighteenth century.[9] A market was held in the nineteenth century, weekly on a Thursday.[10]

North-east of the Square, on the north side of Barrhill Road, is the site of the town's second burial ground. It became the official graveyard after the closure of the original one beside the church in the mid eighteenth century. Burials had, however, taken place at this place previously, as this was also the site of the gallows. This area was often referred to as 'Gallows Hill'. A number of Covenanters were executed here in the 1680s and then buried beside the gallows. The celebrated Covenanting preacher, Reverend Alexander Peden, died peacefully in 1686 and was buried at Auchinleck. His body was exhumed and brought to Cumnock for ritual hanging (which was probably never effected), and buried at the foot of the gallows.[11] Memorials to Peden and other Covenanters still stand in the burial ground **H**.

notes

1	Wyntoun, *Orygynale Cronykil*, ii, 487; Warrick, *Old Cumnock*, 63.	5	*RPC*, ix, 91.
2	*Registrum Episcopatus Glasguensis*, i, p lxiv.	6	Warrick, *Old Cumnock*, 258.
		7	Strawhorn, *New History*, 39.
		8	*RPC*, vii, 290.
3	*RRS*, v, no 38.	9	*OSA*, vi, 113.
4	*APS*, viii, 444–5.	10	Groome, *Gazetteer*, ii, 327.
		11	Strawhorn, *New History*, 27–30.

history

archaeology

P

A similar sequence was identified in this test-pit, with 0.25 m of topsoil overlying weathered natural subsoil.

Q

This test-pit was disturbed by the intrusion of live services, but the observed sequence was similar to that in test-pit **O**.

R

A shallow layer of topsoil was revealed, overlying a gravel loam deposit. Weathered natural subsoil was located *c* 0.25 m below the ground surface. Large boulders were visible some 2 m down.

No finds were recovered from any of the test-pits. The level of the natural subsoil, together with the local topography, indicated that there is a natural hollow along the line of Millbank.

Covenanters' graves NS 5703 2027 **H**
Four Covenanters are buried in a railed-off enclosure in Cumnock Old Graveyard, Gallows Knowe. Warrick, *Old Cumnock*, 161–73.

Market Cross NS 5679 2013 **C**
Cumnock market cross stands in the main square of Old Cumnock. Standing on five steps, the shaft is square in section with splayed angles; it supports a square stone sundial and ball-finial. Two sides of the sundial are sculptured with the arms of the Crichtons and the inscription '1703 repaired 1778'. In 1900, the whole edifice was surmounted by a gas lamp, now removed. Warrick, *Old Cumnock*, 301–4.

area 2
New Bridge Street / Tower Street / the Square, east side / Barrhill Road, south side / Townhead Street / Glaisnock Street / Ayr Road **figure 15**

description

At the eastern end of this area, Tower Street curves down the hill towards the Tanyard and the Lugar Water. To the south there has been considerable landscaping and redevelopment. The newly-built health centre, with associated car parking and grounds, extends southwards down to the Glaisnock Water. One old building, a former mill or warehouse, stands isolated at the corner of Elbow Lane and New Bridge Street **A**.

There is a row of eighteenth-century buildings now facing onto the Square **B**, but which originally faced onto the eastern end of Tower Street **C** (nos 1–16 the Square). The blocked-up doorways and windows can clearly be seen. The south side of Tower Street at this point comprises a social club, garages and an electricity sub-station. A short flight of steps climbs up the steep hill from the bridge over the Glaisnock Water to the side of the social club. A path also leads westwards from the bridge, across a grassed area, to Tower Street.

The south bank of the Glaisnock Water is marked by a high stone wall. This also defines the end of the properties that extend back from the Ayr Road to the water. Blocked-up doorways are also visible in the wall, indicating that there was direct access to the Glaisnock. A large car park, which extends westwards from the back of the properties that front onto Glaisnock Street, occupies much of the eastern end of this block. A narrow alley, Waterside, leads from the car park on the south side of the Glaisnock water side, along the side of the water to Glaisnock Street. Remnants of stone walls at the edge of the car park outline where old property boundaries used to be. Many of the buildings on the Ayr Road are currently being renovated on the outside, and no 30–32 **D** in particular is interesting as it shows that the street frontage was originally set further back from its present position.

The eastern side of Glaisnock Street has seen significant redevelopment in recent years, notably the Glaisnock Shopping Precinct and associated car parking **E**. Built in the 1970s it covers a large area between Townhead Street and Glaisnock Street, extending back to the Glaisnock Water.

South of the Glaisnock Water and east of Glaisnock Street is the old gas works and, immediately south of it, the site of the Cumnock Pottery **F**. Established in 1792, it continued in business until 1920.

North of Townhead Street and east of The Strand, there has been some new development including shops and a bank, with flats above. Waste ground to the east of this block serves as temporary car parking for the adjacent shops. There is a narrow strip of ground to the rear of this development, with an electricity sub-station and parking, before the ground rises steeply up to Greenmill Primary School. The Strand continues up the hill from Townhead Street, skirting around the side of the school, before joining up with Barhill Road. On the west side of the Strand, the rear of the tea-room (no 13, formerly the surgery) shows that there has been some terracing into the slope of the hill **G**. Behind the tea-room is a small area of open ground in front of a commercial garage.

The final block within Area 2 comprises those buildings fronting onto the eastern end of the Square and the western end of Townhead Street. The Royal and Mercat Hotels face onto the Square, with a narrow close running north to south behind them **H**. There are two elevated walkways connecting the hotels, which have extensions to the rear. The building at the north end of the close is currently in use as a garage; beyond this is the playground of Greenmill Primary School.

The western end of Townhead Street, at its junction with Glaisnock Street (nos 1–11 Townhead Street and 15–17 Glaisnock Street), is one of the more interesting areas of the town. The buildings, some currently being refurbished on the outside, are tightly packed together, with a small alley to the rear. The concentration of old inns in this once cramped corner adds character to the town.

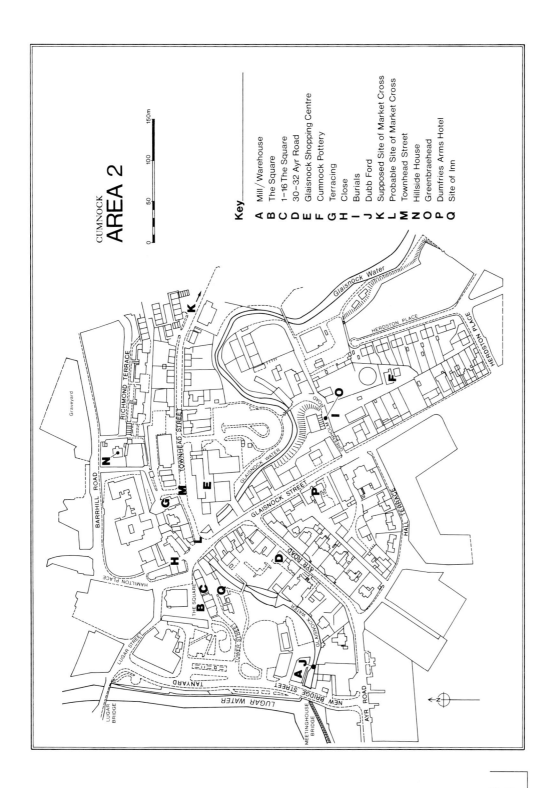

CUMNOCK
AREA 2

0   50   100   150m

Key

A Mill/Warehouse
B The Square
C 1–16 The Square
D 30–32 Ayr Road
E Glaisnock Shopping Centre
F Cumnock Pottery
G Terracing
H Close
I Burials
J Dubb Ford
K Supposed Site of Market Cross
L Probable Site of Market Cross
M Townhead Street
N Hillside House
O Greenbraehead
P Dumfries Arms Hotel
Q Site of Inn

figure 15
Area 2

On the opposite side of the street, at the corner of Glaisnock Street and Tower Street, are a group of buildings that have been built directly over the Glaisnock Water (nos 2–10 Glaisnock Street), although no 2, a bookmaker's, has been heavily altered and much of this building is of twentieth-century construction.

historical background

Tower Street, or Back Street, was the traditional entry from the west into Cumnock. From Stepends Ford in the north-west (by the now Lugar Bridge), the path to the town centre dog-legged south down Back Vennel to enter Tower Street. From the south, the Glaisnock Water was crossed by Dubb Ford **J**, and Tower Street approached by Townfoot. Originally the buildings along Tower Street fronted onto the street, not facing the Square as they do now. A number of merchant shops were sited in this street,[1] as was the Blue Tower Inn. Inns and hostelries were significant landmarks in Cumnock. Being at the intersection of two routeways—Ayr and the west to Edinburgh and the east, and Glasgow and the north to the Borders and the south—Cumnock was host to travellers, whether on foot, by stage-coach or later by train. The Blue Tower Inn on occasion served as the local gaol, the Reverend David Houston being warded here while in custody prior to being taken to Edinburgh by government dragoons in 1688.[2]

The siting of merchant shops in Tower Street would suggest that the market was held nearby. Tradition has it, however, that the market cross was sited at the far, easterly, end of Townhead Street, where there is now a marker on the ground **K**. Such a position would be highly unusual. The market was the hub of urban life and early settlement clustered around it. The east end of Townhead Street was, on the other hand, somewhat removed from this centre of activities in the sixteenth century, and even until well into the nineteenth century. It is, therefore, an unlikely site for an urban market. A more probable site is at the junction of Tower Street, Townhead Street and, later, the Square **L**. Wherever they were sited, however, markets were certainly a common feature in Cumnock. The right to have a weekly market had been granted in 1509 when the burgh was established;[3]

history

archaeology

archaeological potential and future development

The draft Local Plan of 1994 proposes a number of envronmental improvements for this area, as part of its Town Action Plan, including the prohibition of access from the Square to Glaisnock Street and the provision of additional parking in the area. A number of gap sites are considered ripe for redevelopment, but none is referred to specifically. The 1970s Glaisnock Shopping Precinct along Townhead Street is considered in need of upgrading, and improvements to the appearance of the central area of the town are also anticipated.

Most of the Square **B** falls within Area 1 of this survey, but its southern end falls within Area 2. The Square, with its sixteen listed buildings, is a designated Conservation Area. It must also be seen as an archaeologically sensitive area of primary importance within the burgh. This is the site of both the early medieval church and associated graveyard, of which little is known. The extent to which the underlying archaeological material has been damaged by improvements from the mid eighteenth century onwards is difficult to assess at this stage, in the absence of any previous archaeological work. Although development here is unlikely in the foreseeable future, any further environmental improvements must be archaeologically assessed.

The frontages, both around the Square and of the major streets within the historic core of the town, particularly the Townhead area and the close behind the Royal and Mercat Hotels **H**, must also remain a priority. Here, sealed below the foundations, remains of the very earliest settlement in the burgh may survive, in the form of timber buildings. Significant sections of the Tower Street and Townhead Street frontages have been lost, but the remains of earlier building foundations, including the site of the Blue Tower Inn **J**, may still survive below ground. A cellar study was beyond the scope of this survey but, particularly along the main street frontages, approximately half the properties would be

and it is clear that markets were still being held in the early seventeenth century.⁴ They had died out, probably because of the growing number of retail shops, by the late eighteenth century.⁵ A market was held again in the nineteenth century, weekly on a Thursday.⁶

The marker at Townhead Street possibly pinpoints the site of the Cumnock fair, once held by Stepends Ford, but moved in the mid eighteenth century because of development in that area (*see* p 15). The burghal charter had granted the right to an annual fair, and this was extended in 1681 to three a year.⁷ Such occasions would attract not only the Cumnock residents and their neighbours from the surrounding rural hinterland, but also traders from further afield. In the eighteenth and nineteenth centuries, a traditional accompaniment to the spring fair was the horse race. How early this event had begun in Cumnock is unclear, but it may have been of some antiquity, as there is reference to a horse race run in the town in 1610.⁸

Townhead Street **M** (*see* **figure 5**) was to become noted as a centre of the town's weaving industry. By 1811 Cumnock housed seventy muslin weavers and by the 1830s there were more than 120 looms in the town. In Townhead Street virtually every house had at least one loom, six had four looms and three had six.⁹

Standing north of Townhead Street, approached by way of the Strand, on Barrhill Road was Hillside House **N**, an imposing villa. This was the home of the Crichtons, two of whom are remembered in the Crichton Memorial Church (*see* p 44). For a number of years from 1864 onwards, the Strand housed, in an old tree, the bell of the demolished parish church **figure 20**. This was rung twice a day and also on Sundays for worship until it was removed to the public school.

Glaisnock Street was an eighteenth-century addition to the Cumnock town plan **figure 11**. Access in this direction was facilitated by the building of a bridge across the Glaisnock **figure 7**, thus creating a more direct route to New Cumnock and to Ayr by the Ayr Road, which joined Glaisnock Street. The Ayrshire Turnpike Acts of 1766 and 1774, as well as the improvements to parish roads effected by the Earl of Dumfries, encouraged upgrading and maintenance of roadways, to facilitate travel by coach. To assist in the maintenance of

history

archaeology

expected to have cellars; cellared properties are less likely to have archaeological remains preserved beneath them.

Other than the historic standing buildings, there is little physical evidence—in the form of existing property boundaries—to indicate the layout of the medieval burgage plots in this part of the town. Cartographic evidence indicates that the burgh was a patchwork of small gardens or burgage plots, but, sadly, none survive within Area 2. These are often invaluable to the urban archaeologist, as evidence may survive of medieval garden soils, rubbish pits or middens, all of which provide evidence for the date and nature of earlier land use. Areas of waste ground behind frontages may still yield this sort of information, and should therefore routinely be assessed archaeologically in advance of any proposed ground disturbance.

The area between Townhead Street and Glaisnock Street has seen considerable redevelopment and landscaping in recent years. Within the footprint of the shopping centre itself **E**, any archaeological deposits are likely already to have been destroyed. Archaeological evidence, in the form of burgage plots that extended back from Townhead Street for instance, may however still survive underneath the landscaped areas and car parks around the shopping centre.

South of the Glaisnock Water there is some archaeological potential. The area once known as Greenbraehead is the supposed site of a number of burials **I** (*see below*), victims of an epidemic in 1600. Immediately south of this is the site of the Cumnock pottery **F**, established in 1792. Remains of the kilns and quantities of waste material may be preserved below ground.

The west side of Glaisnock Street, south of the river, has mainly been turned over to car parking. This may also be a slightly later phase of settlement or suburb and perhaps has limited archaeological potential.

these roads, dues were collected at toll gates. The hinges of the gate that stood at the entry of Ayr Road to Glaisnock Street were visible until the early twentieth century. It was a practice to erect triumphal archways to celebrate special occasions in many towns. Old photographs show one in Cumnock, on Glaisnock Street **figure 11**. Arches like this were probably erected on occasions such as the marriages, or returns to the burgh, of the Earls of Dumfries.

On the east side of Glaisnock Street is Greenbraehead **O**, the site of the burial of the town's plague victims in 1600.[10] Although the official burial ground was beside the church (*see* p 14), the death-rate was such that a further burial ground had to be found. This site may have been chosen because of its distance from habitation at that time—which would show how little Cumnock had expanded from its urban nucleus.

To the south of this site was the Cumnock pottery **F**. Two unsuccessful attempts at establishing pottery works had already been made in the town before Lady Dumfries, in 1792, established a pottery on this site, under the supervision of James Taylor (*see* pp 19–21). Although it was not successful in its original broad remit, it continued into the nineteenth century as a small producer of country brownware pottery, using local clays.

On the other side of Glaisnock Street stands the Dumfries Arms Hotel, once called the

history

New Inn **P**. It was considered of sufficient importance to appear prominently on the 1770s

archaeology

Street improvements may also reveal features sealed beneath the road surface itself. Evidence for some of the earlier bridges over the Glaisnock Water may survive underneath the Glaisnock Street/Townhead Street junction. Other features that may be preserved include earlier street levels and features which predate the construction of the street itself. Perhaps most importantly, the original site of the market cross has still to be confirmed; a prime candidate for its original location may be at the junction of Townhead Street and Glaisnock Street. Archaeological investigation here, in advance of any street improvements undertaken, may be able to confirm this hypothesis.

As a footnote, a Bronze Age cist and a Roman coin were found somewhere in this area, but no accurate find spots are recorded (*see below*). The possible survival of prehistoric archaeology must therefore be taken into account, both in this area and elsewhere within the historic core of Cumnock.

chance finds and other features

Although no archaeological work has been carried out to date anywhere in Cumnock, and no bore-hole surveys have been carried out in this area for which the results are publicly available, several chance finds have been reported from Area 2.

Armstrongs' map of Ayrshire **figure 8**. Cumnock stood at the crossing of the major east–west and north–south routes (*see* p 5). The New Inn, where Walter Scott once spent the night, was one of several hostelries catering for travellers.

The other inns stood nearer the centre of the town. The Black Bull Inn, now called The Mercat, was a well-known hostelry, catering for coach travellers and, from the mid nineteenth century, for rail passengers. This hotel stood to the east side of the Square. The original entrance to the properties on this side of the Square may, as with the other sides, have faced onto the back lane or close **H** which was, before the opening of the Square to traffic, the main thoroughfare northwards to the manse and the Barrhill Road. Nearby stood the Royal Hotel, the Craighead Inn and the Glaisnock Inn.

notes

1	Strawhorn, *New History*, 33.		6	Groome, *Gazetteer*, ii, 327.
2	*Ibid*, 29.		7	*APS*, viii, 444–5.
3	*RRS*, v, no 38.		8	*RPC*, ix, 91.
4	*RPC*, vii, 290.		9	Strawhorn, *New History*, 52.
history	5	*OSA*, vi, 113.	10	*Ibid*, 30.

archaeology

burials NS 570 199 **I**
An epidemic, the exact nature of which is unknown, broke out in Cumnock in 1600. Many who died were not buried in the churchyard, but at the small piece of ground called Greenbraehead, overlooking the Glaisnock Water. Warrick, *Old Cumnock*, 333–4.

Roman coin, Cumnock (no national grid reference recorded)
A denarius of Faustina II was found somewhere in the Cumnock district many years ago by a local resident. A.S. Robertson, *PSAS*, xciv (1960–61), 138.

Bronze Age cist burial NS 57 20
A collared Cinerary urn, exhibited at Glasgow in 1911, was found in a cist in Cumnock. It is now held in Glasgow Art Gallery and Museum. I.H. Longworth, *Collared Urns of the Bronze Age in Great Britain and Ireland* (Cambridge, 1984), 309.

Site of inn NS 5681 2010 **R**
The Blue Tower Inn, built in 1666, was for many years the principal inn in the town; Tower Street derived its name from this inn. J Warrick, *History of Old Cumnock* (1899), 176.

the archaeological potential of Cumnock a summary **figure 22**

an overview

Like many of the historic burghs in Scotland, Cumnock has experienced a great deal of redevelopment in recent years and, in particular, landscaping. An earlier phase of redevelopment took place in the mid eighteenth century, when the Square was remodelled. The extent of the survival of archaeological deposits or earlier features of the townscape is presently almost completely unkown since, to date, there has been no opportunity to carry out any archaeological fieldwork in the burgh.

On the whole, the potential for the preservation of archaeological deposits within the medieval core of Cumnock is perhaps limited. Nevertheless, routine monitoring and excavations in many other Scottish towns, especially Perth and Aberdeen but also in some smaller towns, have demonstrated that medieval and later archaeological remains do often survive beneath a modern street frontage. Therefore, the site of any proposed redevelopment or ground disturbance along the main street frontages, in particular Townhead Street, the frontages around the Square and the Square itself, must be accorded a high archaeological priority, and arrangements should be made for the site to be assessed, monitored and, if necessary, excavated in advance of the development scheme. Similarly, any proposed ground disturbance of the streets and closes themselves (for instance, for essential repairs, access to services, or environmental improvements) should also be monitored routinely, because the remains of one of the most important features of the medieval townscape, the market cross—of which no archaeological evidence exists as yet—and perhaps other features too, may survive beneath them.

Of necessity, this assessment has been made in the almost complete absence of evidence from previous archaeological work in the burgh. The few engineers' bore-holes for which results are available have also been of limited value. Thus, the conclusions and recommendations expressed here should be regarded as provisional. This survey will require periodic review in the light of results from any future campaigns of archaeological fieldwork (assessment, monitoring and excavation), and from other types of sub-surface investigations.

It is important to stress here that the survey area was limited to the core of historic (medieval) Cumnock. There is a recognised, though unquantifiable, potential for the discovery of prehistoric and Roman archaeological remains, both within and outwith the confines of the historic burgh. This potential, demonstrated by the previous chance finds of Bronze Age burials and a Roman coin in the town, is *not* considered or shown on **figure 22**.

Finally, the potential for archaeological features and deposits to be preserved both beneath the floors and within the structures of historic standing buildings in Cumnock (pp 41–4) must not be forgotten. The archaeological potential of Cumnock's historic standing buildings is also *not* shown on **figure 22**, but should be borne in mind when restoration works or other improvements are proposed for these buildings. *The potential of some individual buildings is considered in the next section.*

Turning to the specific areas of Cumnock (as identified in this survey), parts of both Areas 1 and 2 are recognised as having some archaeological potential. **figure 22** defines those parts of the burgh with archaeological potential (shaded green); **all green areas should be treated as potentially archaeologically sensitive**. The market cross itself, shaded red, is a Scheduled Ancient Monument and is protected by law. Effectively redeveloped areas (shaded blue) are probably archaeologically sterile, but pockets of archaeological deposits could be preserved even within areas of apparently low potential.

area 1

The Square, the buildings fronting onto it and the main street frontages, almost certainly offer the best potential for archaeology in the burgh. Area 1 also promises the best preserved backlands—the only burgage plots to survive in the town lie to the north of Lugar Street. To the west of Bank Lane, and between Tower Street and Lugar Street, some evidence of the post-medieval tanning industry may have survived the landscaping of the area.

area 2

As with Area 1, the best potential for archaeology in Area 2 is probably concentrated around the Square, the buildings fronting onto it and the main street frontages, notably the western end of Townhead Street. The original site of the market cross may have been in this area.

Landscaping and new development south of both Tower Street and Townhead Street have probably destroyed much of the archaeology in these areas, but traces of the burgage plots may survive in places. South of the Glaisnock Water, late sixteenth-century burials and remains of the originally late eighteenth-century Cumnock pottery may survive.

figure 16
Parish church

figure 17
Tower Street

historic buildings
and their
archaeological
potential

A few historic standing buildings and thoroughfares serve as reminders of Cumnock's historic past. Archaeological material is likely to be preserved both beneath and within these standing buildings. It may survive either as a sequence of floor levels or as deposits which predate the construction of the buildings themselves, or concealed within the upstanding structures, hidden by later changes.

In the centre of the town *the Square* **figures 6, 14.A** & **18**, now partially pedestrianised, and the parish church retain much of their earlier character. The Square was originally the kirkyard and burial ground of Cumnock; but in the mid eighteenth century a decision was taken to cut a new roadway through it (*see* p 17). The tombstones and human remains were removed, leaving an open area, which as well as providing access for wheeled vehicles, could also function as the meeting place for local events, such as the hiring fairs for farm labourers **figure 9**.

The *parish church* now standing **figures 14.B** & **16** was built in 1867. On its north side is the family vault of the Marquesses of Bute (Earls of Dumfries), at whose expense the church was built. It replaced an old parish church which was built in 1754. This, in its turn, was on the site of the original parish church, which was in existence before Cumnock became a burgh in 1509. This older church is to be seen prominently on early maps of the area, as it was the focal point of the burgh **figure 16**. Although major development here is unlikely, any alterations involving ground disturbance within the standing building, for example the insertion of new services, may reveal remains of the 1754 structure which the present church replaced, or even of the earlier medieval church, of which so little is known.

Standing to the south of the parish church is the old *market cross* **figure 14.C**, the only Scheduled Ancient Monument in Cumnock. This is not its original position (*see* pp 51–2 and **figures 14.N** & **15.K/L**). Its first site may have been in Townhead Street, but in the eighteenth century it was transferred to, or first erected at the north-east corner of the Square, from where it was moved to ease access in that area. Topped with a sundial, it bears the arms and motto of the earls of Dumfries and the dates '1703 repaired 1778' **figure 4**.

Flanking the Square are a number of old buildings, recalling much of the character of eighteenth-century Cumnock, although not all were constructed as early as this **figure 18**. To the south, *3–14 the Square* **figure 15.C**, is an especially complete range of eighteenth-century houses, probably the finest surviving group in Ayrshire, standing on the site of earlier merchant houses and shops. One, now a shoe repairers and kebab and pizza house, retains its Victorian panelled pilasters and modillioned cornice. The houses' rears face on to what used to be called Tower Street **figure 17**.

Some of the buildings around the Square post-date the abandonment of the graveyard in the mid eighteenth century. If the building line of these encroached onto the earlier graveyard, there is a possibility that burials may be preserved, sealed beneath their floor levels .

On other sides of the Square, old inns are reminders of Cumnock's role as a market centre for the rural surroundings and as a resting place for travellers using either the east-west route between Edinburgh and Ayr, or the north-south route from Glasgow to Carlisle. To the west is the eighteenth-century two-storeyed *Sun Inn*; and to the east, the *Mercat* is the old Black Bull Hotel with its eighteenth-century core, but the recessed, central three-storeyed portion of which belongs to the early nineteenth century. On the south-east corner, the *Craighead Inn*, remodelled in the nineteenth century, stands with its gable end to the bridge over the Glaisnock.

Recent excavations in comparable burghs elsewhere have shown that street frontages are normally the most rewarding areas to investigate, despite the problem of cellarage. Although there has been no opportunity to examine any of the street frontages in Cumnock, evidence of medieval and early post-medieval structures in the form of post-holes and floor surfaces may be expected, sealed beneath the eighteenth- or nineteenth-century standing buildings. Recent excavations in Perth, Dunfermline and Arbroath have also shown that the widths and alignments of the main streets in burghs have changed

42

figure 18
The Square

figure 19
Lugar Street

over the centuries, sometimes considerably. Earlier cobbled street surfaces and contemporary buildings may be preserved up to three or four metres behind the line of the modern street frontages.

Moving north-east out of the Square, Barrhill Road leads to the erstwhile site of the gallows and the *graveyard* **figure 14.H** which superseded the old kirkyard. It houses a number of interesting monuments, including one erected in 1891 in memory of Reverend Alexander Peden (1626-86) (*see* p 16). The *Lugar Bridge* (or Stepends Bridge) **figure 14.K**, over which traffic crossed the Lugar to enter the Square via Lugar Street **figure 19** at the north-west, is an early nineteenth-century structure, replacing an original stone one built in the eighteenth century. It was near here that the Stepends Ford originally gave access to the town.

Along the road to Auchinleck stand two houses of interest: *Lochnorris*, built in 1891, was the home of Keir Hardie and his family; and a little further along, *Broomfield*, now the premises of the local rugby club, is an attractive two-storeyed house, with one-storeyed supporting wings. It is a reminder of some of the prestigious housing built in and around the town in the late eighteenth and nineteenth centuries. Typical of smaller houses of the same period, three properties stand on the east side of the Lugar Bridge. *Riverside*, the nearest to the river bank, is an attractive late eighteenth-century house set back from the road. Beside it, two properties at *14 Lugar Street* **figure 14.F**, regrettably due for demolition, are also reminders of late eighteenth-century Cumnock's quality dwellings. Nearby, off Lugar Street, a larger property, built in the mid nineteenth century, retains many classical features, such as the consoled doorpiece and cornice. Now functioning as *Strathclyde Regional Council Area Office*, it has unfortunately undergone some reglazing which detracts from the attractiveness of the building.

A little to the north, the former *manse* stands in Robertson Avenue **figure 14.I**, on the site of the medieval manse. This is the sole reminder of the medieval manse and glebe, the latter now under housing. Although converted into flats and with many later additions, the oldest part to the north, dating to around 1750, is still discernible.

Another standing eighteenth-century building is the *Dumfries Arms Hotel* in Glaisnock Street **figure 15.P**. The original inn on this site was called the New Inn, and is clearly visible on, for example, Thomson's map of Ayrshire. In spite of many later alterations and additions, a remnant of the Dumfries Arms, once a renowned hotel, is still visible. Along with those at the Square, it afforded a resting-place for travellers by coach and, later, by train. It was here that Walter Scott stayed while passing through Cumnock (*see* p 18).

Glaisnock Street once had a number of attractive buildings **figure 11**. Few now remain. *Nos 12–16* and *20–24 Glaisnock Street*, a good run of prosperous Victorian commercial properties, display evidence of early nineteenth-century doorpieces and cornices on their façades, while functioning now as café, shops and Chinese restaurant. Number 18, the *Glaisnock Inn*, a two-storeyed building with attics above, is of later nineteenth-century origin, with a centre arched and keyblocked doorpiece and two bipartite bays at the first floor, architraved with cornices. On the other side of the street is another late nineteenth-century building. *Nos 61* and *63 Glaisnock Street* may have been designed as quality business chambers. Alterations at ground floor have removed some of the early features, and the upper left window is blocked, but it is possible to see, in the corniced wallhead, the sash and case windows, coped gabletted skews and finialled gables, the remnants of a distinguished building.

Further along Glaisnock Street, the *Town Hall* is also a late nineteenth-century building. A two-storeyed red ashlar building with three-bayed front, it is a monument to the civic pride of Cumnock. The town had long felt the lack of a public meeting hall; halls connected with the school, the United Presbyterian Church, the Black Bull Hotel and the Dumfries Arms had all served in this capacity. Although the Marquess of Bute provided the site and a sum of £500 towards its construction, public subscriptions raised over £2,000; a concert and ball, prior to the opening on 7 January 1885, raised a further £70; and the shortfall was made up by a bazaar held in 1896. Fittingly, in front of it is Benno Schotz' fine bust of Keir Hardie, 1939, Cumnock's famous son.

The *Royal Bank of Scotland*, Glaisnock Street and the *Bank of Scotland* on the corner of Glaisnock Street and Ayr Road, built in 1866 and 1870 respectively to the architectural designs of Peddie and Kinnear, are fine examples of banking halls. The Bank of Scotland building, now the offices of R.A. Logan and Co., solicitors, is in Scottish baronial style, three-storeyed, with dormer heads, a splayed corner entrance with corbelled turret over and crow-stepped gables. The Royal Bank has a central doorway with moulded round-headed doorcase with a fanlight and hoodmould, and to the sides projecting bipartite windows. A building on the site of the former parish school in the Square was acquired by the Ayrshire Banking Company in 1834 and subsequently by the Western Bank of Scotland in 1845. Twelve years later it became the premises of the *Clydesdale Bank*. A substantial building of two storeys, with attics, it has an arched doorway and pedimented masonry dormers. All of these buildings reflect the growing status of the burgh in the nineteenth century.

Standing churches are a clue to nineteenth-century attitudes in Cumnock. The *United Presbyterian Church*, now Strathclyde Regional Supplies Department, was built in 1831 as the Cumnock Associate Church (Burgher) on the site of an earlier church of 1775. It is rectangular, with an unusual three-bay façade facing westwards to the Tanyard. The

44

figure 20

The bell from
the old parish church

central entrance bay is framed by two windows with lattice glazing. Its appearance is marred by the more northerly window now being blocked and the southerly one being partially built up. Nearby stands the *Crichton Memorial Church*. Its origins also lay in dissent. From 1843, some parishioners worshipped independently as the Free Church. In 1896 this building was presented by Miss Crichton of Hillside House (*see* p 35; **figure 15.N**) in memory of her father and brother. Built of red/pink sandstone, it is in Victorian Gothic style with an impressive 140-foot (42.7 m) steeple. Its first minister was John Warrick, the local historian.

Cumnock *Congregational Church* is at Stepends on the north side of Stepends or Lugar Bridge. The Congregationalists originally met in a hall in the Black Bull Hotel from 1838 and then transferred to a chapel in the Square, on the site of the old school **figure 14.L**. By 1882/3, however, this new church was opened for worship. Keir Hardie was for a while associated with it, before the pastor and thirty-seven members established a separate congregation attached to the Evangelical Union. The church still stands in a relatively unchanged, and seemingly peaceful state, a manse now attached on the north-east side. At the far end of the town, on Glaisnock Street, is the Roman Catholic *Church of St John*. Prior to the erection of this building, Catholic worship had taken place in the parish of Auchinleck and later in halls and a house in Cumnock itself. As a result of the generosity of the third Marquess of Bute, a convert to Roman Catholicism, the church was not only established in 1882, but also maintained by him in its initial years. Designed originally to have been a more impressive structure, with a steeple, its interior is beautifully appointed. It also had the distinction of being the first ecclesiastical building in Britain to have electric lighting.

Outside Cumnock, on the Ayr Road, stands *Bankend Farm*. Although now derelict and boarded up, it still reveals some of the qualities of a substantial agricultural property with close associations with the town. Built in 1855, it is a three-storeyed dwelling with a basement. It has a three-windowed coursed whinstone facade, with raised quoins at angles and openings. The doorpiece has a consoled cornice. The original decorative chimney

figure 21

Glaisnock viaduct
under construction

pots and chimney heads are still in evidence, although the original glazing is obscured and the driveway across which stood a walled and railed garden is scarcely recognisable. The steading, which had finialled gables, is now a ruin.

Also close by Cumnock are two impressive railway viaducts: *Bank Viaduct* and *Glaisnock Viaduct*. The railway to Cumnock was opened in 1850 by the Glasgow, Paisley, Kilmarnock and Ayr Railway Company, after the construction of this bridge over the Lugar Water. Twenty-two years later the Glasgow and South Western Railway Company built a second railway line through Cumnock, called the Ayr and Cumnock branch line, and opened the Glaisnock Viaduct **figure 21**. From the Middle Ages, Cumnock had been strategically placed on crossing routes, whether for foot passengers or, later, coach traffic; this function was maintained by the opening of these lines, viaducts and Cumnock's two railway stations.

Dumfries House, west of Cumnock, would rarely have been seen by the Cumnock townspeople. Yet it had a profound impact on their lives, as it was here that the Earls of Dumfries made their residence from 1759. A spectacular mansion house, it was designed by John and Robert Adam soon after the death of their father, William, who was originally intended to do the designs. The main block, in classical style, is 95 by 65 feet (29 by 20 m), with supporting wings. The Adams also arranged for items made by Sheraton and Chippendale to be sent from London to furnish the interior. From this sumptuous residence the Earls of Dumfries managed their estates and cultivated their intimate links with Cumnock.

further work

gazetteer

Full use has been made in this survey of all primary source material in the national repositories. Unfortunately, however, access to documentation in Dumfries House was not granted at the time of preparation of this survey. Although the work of John Strawhorn, whose publications are cited above, was based on these archives, different questions would have been asked of the source material for the purposes of this survey. It is, therefore, strongly recommended that a full assessment of the primary documentation in Dumfries House should be made as soon as possible, so that a full understanding of the built environment of Cumnock can be gained.

In due course, the historical and documentary evidence for Cumnock's relationship with neighbouring burghs, especially Auchinleck, might usefully be explored.

---

archaeological objectives for the future

Preparation of the Cumnock burgh survey has highlighted a number of directions for future archaeological work. These can be broadly divided into management objectives, priorities for future fieldwork, and other areas which merit further research. Any such list cannot be exhaustive but it should cover the main areas of concern in the foreseeable future.

management objectives

1   Wherever possible, it is important to continue to monitor the impact of any development (in its broadest sense) on the potential archaeological resoiurce (the green areas on **figure 22**). This will require the routine provision of site-specific desk-based assessments, through to watching briefs, trial excavations and, where necessary, controlled excavation, post-excavation analysis and publication. Over time, the cumulative results will 'calibrate' this assessment of the archaeological potential of the burgh, providing evidence about the burgh's origins, and its physical, economic and social development through the centuries.

2   Developments should similarly be monitored to shed more light on the prehistory of Cumnock and on its place in the Roman sphere of influence.

3   The degree and nature of cellarage along the main street frontages was not systematically examined during preparation of this report. Accurate information about cellarage would be useful to managers/curators of the archaeological resource in assessing the archaeological potential of the main street frontages in the historic burgh.

4   Engineers' bore-holes offer a convenient glimpse of the depth and nature of sub-surface deposits, man-made or not, ancient and modern. It would be useful if the results obtained from engineers' bore-holes in and around the core of the historic burgh could be gradually collected and collated. It can be difficult to access all bore-hole results, especially those in the hands of private contractors, and it might be worth considering mechanisms by which such information could more easily (and preferably routinely) be made available to managers/curators of the archaeological resource.

5   Periodic review and updating of this survey would be desirable to take account of the results of any future archaeological work, and of the comprehensive collection and collation of other types of sub-surface investigations eg engineers' bore-holes, systematic survey of cellarage on the main street frontages etc. In particular, the

colour-coded map **figure 22** could perhaps be revised and re-issued at appropriate intervals.

6   Opportunities should continue to be taken to increase public awareness of the potential archaeological interest of Cumnock, both generally, and within the fabric of and beneath historic standing buildings. This survey represents an important first step in this direction.

priorities for future fieldwork

So little archaeological work has so far been undertaken in Cumnock that the priorities for the future are fairly rudimentary. However, the following priorities should be borne in mind when assessing the possible archaeological impact of any development proposals, and during the preparation of any archaeological project designs.

1   Define the limits of the early settlement and later development of Cumnock. Were the Lugar and Glaisnock Waters, and the 125 m OD contour to the east, limiting factors in the development of the settlement?

2   Identify any sequence of planning in the layout and expansion of the burgh, and determine any variation in street alignment and width.

3   Test the hypothesis of this survey that the original site of the market cross (and market place) was at the west end of Townhead Street, at its junction with Glaisnock Street; if not, ascertain its original location.

4   Assess the nature of the burgage plots to the north of Lugar Street, and determine whether they are contemporary with the founding of the burgh.

5   Identify the site and date of the construction of the early church, and subsequent later phases. Investigate the extent of the old churchyard that existed in the Square until the eighteenth century, and locate any physical boundaries to it.

6   Examine the archaeological remains of Cumnock's industrial heritage—in particular, tanning, cotton-weaving and pottery making.

areas for further archaeological research

1   Examine the pre-1500 medieval landscape in the vicinity of Cumnock—notably the possible mottes at Mote Hill and Castle Hill and any associated land divisions— to establish the context for the founding of the burgh.

gazetteer of previous archaeological work and chance finds
from in and around Cumnock

This gazetteer of previous archaeological work and chance finds from Cumnock and its immediate environs is based on the National Monument Record of Scotland's database; this should be consulted for further references.

the prehistoric and Roman period

Bronze Age burials NS 5855 1738
A number of urns have been found since the early nineteenth century in a sand and gravel pit at the south-west of 'Castle Hill' near Borland Mill. Steven notes that in 1849 'a number of ancient urns' were recovered, with one urn containing the calcined bones of a child. Warrick then mentions that two urns were found in the Spring of 1898 'in a sandhill close to Borland Mill'. A piece of charred wood was found beside them, and both were half-filled with calcined bones. In 1938 fragments of a collared Cinerary Urn were found in the same sand pit, and excavations the following year revealed a layer of ash and fragments of burnt bone. A beaker sherd was also picked up nearby in 1939. The excavations also revealed a wood-lined shaft, possibly a refuse dump for Borland Castle (*see* Borland—'Castle Hill' below). A number of references exist for these discoveries, including: A G M'Leod, *PSAS*, lxxiv (1939–40), 136–7; H J Steven, *Old Cumnock* (1899), 102; Warrick, *Old Cumnock*, 14.

Cumnock NS 57 20
Bronze Age cist burial A collared Cinerary Urn, exhibited at Glasgow in 1911, was found in a cist at Cumnock. It is now held in Glasgow Art Gallery and Museum. I H Longworth, *Collared Urns of the Bronze Age in Great Britain and Ireland* (Cambridge, 1984), 309.

Lugar, Chapel Knowe NS 5909 2129
Bronze Age burial Paterson suggests that a pre-Reformation chapel stood on Chapel Knowe, which lies above a low terrace of the Lugar Water. He adds that the knoll was probably a tumulus as 'a small urn, containing bones', was found by workmen excavating for the Lugar iron works (in 1846). Chapel Knowe has since been totally defaced, and only a large tree remains to mark its site. J Paterson, *History of the Counties of Ayr and Wigtown*, vol i, part 1 (Edinburgh, 1863), 182.

Sykeside Bridge NS 5878 1913
Metalwork There is a nineteenth-century reference to sword points, spearheads and hilts of swords of 'curious metal' having been found in and around the Sykeside Bridge area, which today lies on the railway route. NMRS Record Card RCAHMS NS 51 NE2.

Auchinleck, Main Street NS 55 21
Roman coin A worn bronze coin of Constans Caesar (AD 337–350), minted at Antioch, was found 1 foot (0.3 m) below ground while digging in the garden of a house in Main Street, Auchinleck. A S Robertson, *PSAS*, xciv (1960–61), 138.

Cumnock no NGR
Roman coin A rare denarius of Faustina II, wife of emperor Marcus Aurelius (AD 161–180), was found somewhere in the Cumnock district many years ago by a local resident. A S Robertson, *PSAS*, xciv (1960–61), 138.

the medieval and later periods

Borland Castle NS 5864 1742
Site of castle The site of this castle lies some 3.2 km south-east of Cumnock. The building itself no longer exists although its ruins were extant up until at least 1847. The castle belonged to the Montgomeries in 1400 and remained occupied until the late seventeenth century. No trace of any building could be seen by the Ordnance Survey Archaeological

Division surveyor in 1981. Warrick states that 'occasionally the plough strikes the foundation'. The approximate line of foundations struck during ploughing were pointed out to the surveyor by the farmer in 1981. Warrick, *Old Cumnock*, 23.

Borland—'Castle Hill' NS 5854 1740

Mound of unknown date. This possible motte lies about 150 m north-east of Borland Castle (*see* above). It is a flat-topped, squarish mound, measuring 64 by 27 m at its base and 48 by 27 m on its upper surface. It may represent the remains of an earthen and timber castle, in which case it was perhaps a predecessor to the stone-built Borland Castle. Minor excavations between 1938–9 in a sand and gravel pit at the south-west of the mound produced evidence of Bronze Age burials (*see* Bronze Age burials, above); but also a wood-lined shaft, possibly a refuse shaft for Borland Castle, which contained short stakes and wood fragments, a handle of a medieval jug, a sole of a leather shoe or boot, and broken animal bones. D Christison, *PSAS*, xxvii (1892–3), 401; A G M'Leod, *PSAS*, lxxiv (1939–40), 136–7.

Terringzean Castle NS 5556 2048

Remains of castle The castle is situated some 3 km west of Cumnock and within the policies of Dumfries House. Warrick states that it was known at one time as Craufurdstoun, belonging to the Craufurd family before 1467, passing eventually to the Earl of Loudoun and then to the earls of Dumfries. It was described by the *Old Statistical Account* as having been 'in ruins' in 1750.

The castle stands on the lower slopes of a hill overlooking, and within a bend in the Lugar Water. A dry moat defends the north-east and north-west approaches to a single tower or keep. The octagonal ashlar-faced tower dates to the fourteenth century. The walls are 2 m thick and survive to a height of 6 m on the south side. The remains of an ancillary outbuilding lie to the north of the castle. Excavations, carried out by Lord Bute in 1897, exposed only the foundations of later walls. Warrick, *Old Cumnock*, 21–2; D Macgibbon & T Ross *The Castellated and Domestic Architecture of Scotland from the Twelfth to the Eighteenth Century*, v (1892), 352–3.

Mote Hill NS 5755 2069

Possible site of motte and bailey castle Warrick states that the Mote Hill was the place where justice courts were held, implying that it was the seat of the lord of the barony. Surrounded on three sides by the Lugar Water, this natural promontory measures *c* 15–18 m in height, *c* 182 m in length and *c* 15–30 m in breadth. The summit is crowned by a narrow ridge some 1.5 m wide. Steven thought that this natural peninsula was probably the site of a fort, but no defensive features can be seen. Although there is no evidence of medieval occupation, it is possible that this was the site of the original castle of Cumnock. Today the area is heavily wooded. Steven, *Old Cumnock*, 102; Warrick, *Old Cumnock*, 44.

Leifnoreis Castle NS 53 20

Site of castle The castle of Leifnoreis was situated in the grounds of Dumfries House, about 1.5 km west of Terringzean Castle. This castle was first recorded in 1440 and was held by a branch of the Craufuird family. The stone tower house, called the Ward of Leifnoreis, was erected and held by the family until 1650, when it was bought by the earl of Dumfries. It was inhabited possibly until 1757. There were no visible remains of the castle by the end of the nineteenth century. Warrick, *Old Cumnock*, 19.

Cumnock Castle NS 6174 1384

Site of castle This castle, situated some 8 km south of Cumnock in the village of New Cumnock, has been variously known as Black Bog Castle and Black Craig Castle. It was originally the seat of the Dunbars, and is known to have been in existence since at least the early fourteenth century. The castle may have been re-built around the mid seventeenth century.

The *New Statistical Account* of 1845 (v, 517) notes that the earthworks were still in existence, but that the castle had been quarried for its stone around 1800, suggesting substantial remains until then. No trace remains of the actual castle, but a portion of the earthwork on which it stood is still visible. It is possible that this castle succeeded an earlier earthwork, possibly on Mote Hill (*see* above). The parish church of New Cumnock, built in 1650, and other modern buildings have destroyed all trace of it on the east, south and west sides. Warrick, *Old Cumnock*, 44.

Borland Chapel NS 5939 1730
Chapel, burial ground and grave-slab Remains of a pre-Reformation chapel (called 'Hallow Chapel' or 'Borland Chapel' by Warrick) were visible here in 1837, but almost all traces had disappeared by 1899. A stone, thought to be from this chapel and carved with concentric circles, has been built into the wall of Chapel Farmhouse. Human bones, including skulls, found when ploughing or digging here indicate an associated burial ground. Fieldwork conducted by the Ordnance Survey in 1981 suggests that the ridges and furrows around the site are due to relatively recent agricultural activity. A small rectangular structure was noted at NS 5939 1729, but this was considered to be part of the croft. Warrick, *Old Cumnock*, 69–70.

Lugar, Chapel Knowe NS 5909 2129
Possible site of chapel Paterson suggests that a pre-Reformation chapel stood on Chapel Knowe, which lies above a low terrace of the Lugar Water. The eminence called Chapel Knowe has been totally defaced, only a large tree remaining to mark its site. No trace of a mound or structure is visible today. Paterson, *History of Ayr and Wigtown*, i, part 1, 182.

Cumnock NS 570 199
Burials An epidemic, the exact nature of which is not known, broke out in Cumnock in 1600. Many who died from it were not buried in the churchyard, but at the small piece of ground called Greenbraehead, overlooking the Glaisnock. Warrick, *Old Cumnock*, 333–4.

Covenanters' Graves NS 5703 2027
Four Covenanters are buried in a railed-off enclosure in Cumnock Old Graveyard, on Gallows Knowe. Warrick, *Old Cumnock*, 161–73.

Meikle Auchingibbert NS 5925 1943
Single burial John McGeachan, a farmer in Meikle Auchingibbert, was wounded in a skirmish with dragoons on 20 June 1688 at Bellow Path near Lugar. He died of his wounds three weeks later and was buried at this spot. Warrick, *Old Cumnock*, 176–8.

Cumnock NS 5679 2013
Market cross Cumnock market cross, the only Scheduled Ancient Monument in the burgh, today stands in the main square of Old Cumnock **figure 4**. Standing on a five-stage base, the cross shaft is square in section with splayed angles. It is surmounted by a square stone sundial and ball-finial. Two sides of the sundial are sculptured with the arms of the Crichtons and the inscription '1703 repaired 1778'. In 1900, the whole was surmounted by a gas lamp.

This eighteenth-century cross is most unlikely to be the original market cross of Cumnock since the burgh was granted the right to erect a market cross by James IV as early as 1509—almost two centuries earlier than the extant cross. Nor can this eighteenth-century cross occupy the position of the original cross, as this was the site of a graveyard until sometime in the 1760s, when the graveyard was levelled and the graves removed (*see* p 17). The original market cross would certainly not have been erected in a graveyard. The present cross cannot have been placed here earlier than the 1760s.

A chart of unknown date (not seen by the present authors), in the possession of the Marquis of Bute, shows a cross standing at the north-east corner of the Square, just where the Barrhill Road met it (NS 5671 2018) (Hamilton Place did not exist then). Yet this does not seem to be the original site of the cross either. Local tradition states that the cross stood at the west end of the Townhead **figure 15.L**, that is, south-east of the Square. Here, the street is at its narrowest and slopes down towards the old ironstone pit. A causeway of water-worn stones has been inserted at this point; one stone, larger than the others and about '9 inches square', right in the middle of the street, marks the spot where the earlier market cross is said originally to have stood. Warrick, *Old Cumnock*, 301–4.

Cumnock NS 5681 2010
Site of inn The Blue Tower Inn, built in 1666, was for many years the principal inn in the town, and from which Tower Street derived its name. Warrick, *Old Cumnock*, 176.

Meikle Auchingibbert NS 5925 1950
Farmstead Turf-covered footings of an old croft lie some 70 m north of the grave of John McGeachan (NS 5925 1943).

Lugar NS 591 293
Village and ironworks Both the village and the ironworks were established in 1846. J Butt, *Industrial Archaeology in Scotland* (Newton Abbot, 1967), 218.

Auchinleck Road	*Area 1*	The road to the neighbouring burgh of Auchinleck, which crossed the Lugar Water at Stepends Ford.
Ayr Road	*Area 2*	The road to Ayr, leading off Glaisnock Street, was opened up in the late eighteenth century.
Back Street	*Area 2*	This back street once connected Townfoot with Townhead. Also called Tower Street.
Bank Lane	*Areas 1 and 2*	This lane to the west of the Square, which connects Tower Street with Lugar Street, is situated on the edge of a slope.
Barrhill Road	*Area 1*	The road to Barrhill and Muirkirk.
Black Bull Close	*Area 2*	The narrow lane which lies behind the Mercat Hotel. It was named after the old Black Bull Inn (now the Mercat Hotel).
Crossrigs	*Area 2*	Stood at the end of Townhead Street.
Deil's Elbow	*Area 2*	The twisting exit from the Square is likened to a devil's elbow.
Dubb Ford	*Area 2*	The Dubb Ford (named after the Scots word 'dub', meaning a puddle) carried a local road over the Glaisnock Water. This was replaced by a bridge in the mid eighteenth century, when the Tanyard was opened up.
Elbow Lane	*Area 2*	This lane runs eastwards from New Bridge Street towards the Glaisnock Water. The kink in its alignment may explain the name.
Glaisnock Street	*Area 2*	Opened in the late eighteenth century and named after the Glaisnock Water. A bridge was built here in 1775.
Greenbraehead	*Area 2*	This area lies just to the east of Glaisnock Street and south of the bend in the Glaisnock Water. Literally meaning the top of the green slope, it may have been an early burial ground for plague victims. A pottery was established here in 1792.
Lugar Street	*Area 1*	Named after the Lugar Water, this street continues westwards from the Square as Auchinleck Road.
Muirkirk Road	*Area 1*	The eastern end of Barrhill Road leads to Muirkirk.

54

New Bridge Street   *Area 2*

Named after the bridge across the Glaisnock Water, this modern street connects Ayr Road with the Tanyard. Cotton weaving was concentrated along this street and also at Townhead.

Pottery Row   *Area 2*

The Cumnock Pottery, established in 1792 and in business until 1920, was on the east side of the road. Pottery Row is now part of Glaisnock Street.

The Square   *Area 1*

Named after the square graveyard of the parish church, which was situated in the centre of the Square. It was levelled in 1768 to allow access to traffic. The Square was remodelled in the mid nineteenth century, with the building of a new parish church and the demolition of old tenements on the north and east sides. The eighteenth-century market cross is sited on the south side of the Square.

Stepends Ford   *Area 1*

The road to Auchinleck crossed the Lugar in the north-western corner of the burgh at Stepends Ford. A bridge was built here in 1753 and this was replaced by a single-arched bridge in 1864.

The Strand   *Area 2*

This narrow street connects Townhead Street with Barrhill Road.

The Tanyard   *Area 1*

The tanning industry in Cumnock was centred around the Tanyard.

Tower Street   *Area 2*

Previously known as Townfoot and Back Street, Tower Street was named after the Blue Tower Inn, built in 1666 and for many years the principal inn in the town. The site of the inn is shown on **figure 15.Q**.

Townfoot   *Area 2*

Townfoot, the road from Tanyard to Back Street, lies at the foot of the plateau on which the Square stands. It was later named Tower Street.

Townhead Street   *Area 2*

Meaning the top of the town. Cotton weaving was concentrated around Townhead. The fair may have been held at the east end of Townhead Street, after it was moved from its original site near Stepends Ford.

Waterside Place   *Area 2*

This street once skirted the northern bank of the Glaisnock Water. A large shopping centre now stands here.

alderman	Chief burghal officer, sometimes called *prepositus*, later provost.
backlands	The area to the rear of the burgage plot behind the dwelling house on the frontage. Originally intended for growing produce and keeping animals; site of wells and midden heaps. Eventually housed working premises of craftsmen and poorer members of burgh society.
bailies	Burgh officer who performed routine administration, often under an alderman or *prepositus*.
booths	Small open-fronted stalls, sometimes free-standing but often appended to the front of houses lining the street, where merchants and craftsmen sold their goods.
boundaries	*see* burgage plot
burgage plot	A division of land, often of regular size, having been measured out by liners, allocated to a burgess. Once built on, it contained the burgage house on the frontage (*see* frontage) and a backland (*see* backland). In time, with pressure for space, the plots were often subdivided—repletion. Plots were bounded by ditches, wattle fences or stone walls.
burgess	Person who enjoys the privileges and responsibilities of the freedom of the burgh.
close	*see* vennel
cordiners	Leather worker.
craft	Trade.
documentary sources	Written evidence, primary sources being the original documents.
façade	Finished face of a building.
feu	A perpetual lease at a fixed rent; a piece of land so held.
frontage	Front part of burgage plot nearest the street, on which the dwelling was usually built.
gap sites	Burgage plots not built up or 'biggit'; in a modern context, undeveloped space between two buildings.
hinterland	Rural area around a burgh, to which the burgh looked for economic and agricultural support; hinterland likewise dependent on burgh market.
indwellers	Unprivileged, non-burgess dweller in a town.
jougs	Iron neck-rings; the old Scottish pillory.
liner	Burgh officer with responsibility to measure burgage plots and supervise building matters.

merkland	A piece of land, having an annual rented value of one merk at the time of assessment.
midden	Refuse heap near dwelling.
motte and bailey, motte	Earthwork castle formed of a large mound encircled by a ditch or ditches, the mound normally topped by a timber wall enclosing a wooden tower. A bailey (outer enclosure) was sometimes provided to give room for ancillary buildings
natural	The level of subsoil undisturbed by human activity.
pend	Narrow close or walkway between buildings.
prehistory	Period of human history before the advent of writing.
rig	*see* burgage plot
tectonic movements	Displacements in the earth's crust.
toft	*see* burgage plot
tolbooth	The most important secular building; meeting place of burgh council; collection post for market tolls; often housed town gaol.
tolls	Payments for use of burgh market.
tron	Public weigh-beam.
urban nucleus	Original site/s from which the town developed.
vennel	Alley; narrow lane.
volcanic plug	An outcrop of volcanic rock which fills, or plugs, a cavity in the earth's crust.

The Acts of the Parliaments of Scotland, 12 vols, edd T Thomson & C Innes (Edinburgh, 1814–1875).

Bain, J (ed), *Calendar of Documents Relating to Scotland*, 5 vols (Edinburgh, 1881–8, 1986).

Groome, F H, *Ordnance Gazetteer of Scotland: A Survey of Scottish Topography*, vol ii (Edinburgh, 1886).

The New Statistical Account of Scotland, vol v ('Old Cumnock Parish' by Reverend Ninian Bannatyne) (Edinburgh, 1845).

Regesta Regum Scottorum, vol v: *The Acts of Robert I, King of Scots, 1306–1329*, ed A A M Duncan (Edinburgh, 1988).

The Register of the Great Seal of Scotland (Registrum Magni Sigilli Regum Scotorum) 11 vols, edd J M Thomson *et al* (Edinburgh, 1882–1914).

The Register of the Privy Council of Scotland, edd J H Burton *et al*:
First Series, 14 vols (Edinburgh, 1977–98).
Second Series, 8 vols (Edinburgh, 1899–1908).
Third Series, 16 vols (Edinburgh, 1908–).

Registrum Episcopatus Glasguensis, 2 vols, ed C Innes (Maitland Club, 1843).

The Statistical Account of Scotland, 1791–1799, vol vi, *Ayrshire*, ed J Sinclair ('Parish of Old Cumnock' by the Rev T Miller). New Edition edd D J Withrington & I R Grant (Wakefield, 1978).

Wyntoun, Andrew de, *The Orygynale Cronykil of Scotland*, ed D Laing (Edinburgh, 1872).

secondary sources

Anon, *Ancient Monuments of Clydesdale* (Clydesdale District Council, 1989).

Anon, *Cumnock and Doon Valley District Wide Draft Local Plan* (Cumnock and Doon Valley District Council, 1994).

Breeze, D, *The Northern Frontiers of Roman Britain* (London, 1982).

Brown, C J & Shipley, B M, *Soil Survey of Scotland: South-East Scotland. Soil and Land Capability for Agriculture* (The Macaulay Institute for Soil Research, Aberdeen, 1982).

Butt, J, *Industrial Archaeology in Scotland* (Newton Abbot, 1967).

Cameron, I B & Stephenson, D, *The Midland Valley of Scotland* (British Regional Geology, Natural Enviroment Research Council, London, 3rd edn, 1985).

Christison, D, 'On the geographical distribution of certain place-names in Scotland', *PSAS*, xxvii (1892–3).

Crossley, D, *Post-Medieval Archaeology in Britain* (Leicester, 1990).

Darvill, T, *Prehistoric Britain* (London, 1987).

Dick, I M *et al*, *The Cumnock Area* (London, 1975).

Dry, F T & Hipkin, J A, *Land Capability for Forestry in South-East Scotland* (Aberdeen, 1989).

Feachem, R, *Guide to Prehistoric Scotland* (London, 1977).

Hanson, W & Maxwell, G, *Rome's North West Frontier* (Edinburgh, 1983).

Laurenson, J C M, *Cumnock and New Cumnock in Old Picture Postcards* (Cumnock, 1983).

I H Longworth, *Collared Urns of the Bronze Age in Great Britain and Ireland* (Cambridge, 1984).

Lorimer, H, *A Corner of Old Strathclyde* (Glasgow, 1952).

Love, D, *A Pictorial History of Cumnock* (Darvel, 1992).

D MacGibbon & T Ross, *The Castellated and Domestic Architecture of Scotland from the Twelfth to the Eighteenth Century* (Edinburgh, 1887–92).

Maxwell, G S, *The Romans in Scotland* (Edinburgh, 1989).

Moore, J (ed), *Among Thy Green Braes* (Cumnock, 1977).

Morrison, A, *The Bronze Age in Ayrshire* (Ayrshire Archaeological and Natural History Society, Ayrshire Collections, xii, no iv, 1978).

Morrison, A & Hughes, I, *The Stone Ages in Ayrshire* (Ayrshire Archaeological and Natural History Society, 1989).

Paterson, J, *History of the Counties of Ayr and Wigtown*, 2 vols (Edinburgh, 1863).

58

Pryde, G S, *The Burghs of Scotland: a Critical List* (Oxford, 1965).

Quail, G, *The Cumnock Pottery* (Ayrshire Archaeological and Natural History Society, Ayrshire Monographs, no xii, 1993).

Robertson, A S, 'Roman coins found in Scotland, 1951–60', *PSAS*, xciv (1960–61).

Sissons, J, *The Geomorphology of the British Isles: Scotland* (London, 1976).

Steven, H J, *The Cumnocks Old and New: their History and Associations* (Kilmarnock, 1899).

Strawhorn, J, *The New History of Cumnock* (Cumnock, 1966).

Strawhorn, J, 'An introduction to Armstrongs' map', *Ayrshire Archaeological and Natural History Society Journal* (1959).

Strawhorn, J & Andrew, K, *Discovering Ayrshire* (Edinburgh, 1988).

Warrick, J, *The History of Old Cumnock* (London, 1899).

cartographic sources

Adair, J, *A Mape of the Wast of Scotland Containing Clydsdail, Nithsdail, Ranfrew, Shyre of Ayre, and Galloway*, 1685.

Armstrong, A & M, *A New Map of Ayrshire*, 1755.

Blaeu, J, *The Province of Kyle* (Amsterdam, 1654).

'Castles of Scotland' (private property of Robin Macpherson).

Gordon of Straloch, Robert, *Cuningham*, *c* 1640.

Map of Roman Britain, published by the Ordnance Survey (Southampton, 1978).

Ordnance Survey sheet (1:10,000) NS 52 SE, 1986.

Roy, W, 'Military Survey of Scotland' [1747–1755], sheet 4/5.

Thomson, J, *Atlas of Scotland* (Renfrewshire and Ayrshire), 1828.